Still In My Own Lynchtime

Still In My Own Lynchtime © Copyright 2006 Brian Lynch

All rights reserved. No part of this work may be reproduced or stored in an information retrieval system (other than for purposes of review) without prior written permission by the copyright holder.

A catalogue record of this book is available from the British Library

First Edition: December 2006

ISBN: 1-84375-290-5

To order additional copies of this book please visit:
http://www.upso.co.uk/brianlynch

Published by: UPSO Ltd
5 Stirling Road, Castleham Business Park,
St Leonards-on-Sea, East Sussex TN38 9NW United Kingdom
Tel: 01424 853349 Fax: 0870 191 3991
Email: info@upso.co.uk   Web: http://www.upso.co.uk

Still In My Own Lynchtime

by

Brian Lynch

If you can fill the unforgiving minute
With sixtyseconds worth of distance run
Yours is the earth, and everything that's in it
And – which is more – you'll be a Man my son
                              Kipling

UPSO

This book is dedicated to our children,
who gave my life meaning;

and to the memory of Winston Churchill,
who gave me my life.

Contents

	Introduction 1
1	Where's ya bin? * 3
2	Fiddler on the hoof * 10
3	After Beslan (SOAPBOX) 13
4	Becky knows * 17
5	I killed my wife yesterday (STORY) 20
6	All at sea * 28
7	No spud in the fire * 60
8	Eat your heart out Emma Bligh (STORY) 63
9	Laugh at them (SOAPBOX) 72
10	The Globe * 76
11	Some long and winding roads * 80
12	Liz and I (Poem) 85
13	Two birds – one stone (STORY) 88
14	The Mild Bunch * 99
15	Scouting for urchins * 102
16	The lips move (SOAPBOX) 107
17	Power corrupts * 111
18	The other man's grass (STORY) 115

19	Whatever happened to Nipper *	122
20	Somebody owes me a pony *	124
21	The Assassins *	127
22	Dishonour among thieves (STORY)	131
23	Have they closed the tripe mines *	135
24	Whacko! *	138
25	Anyone can make a mistake *	141
26	'ancock, Robin and Capn Jim *	144
27	Gun Law (SOAPBOX)	147
28	Pope Jim *	149
29	American hospitality *	156
30	Hitler tried to kill me *	160
31	If its good enough for the Yanks (SOAPBOX)	163
32	One for the Road (STORY)	165
33	Heroes *	173
34	A bootful of beer *	175
35	Happiest days – no way! *	178
36	Music was not my food of love *	185
37	Swimming on a parquet floor *	190
38	Give us our game back (SOAPBOX)	193
39	On the run, in the bushes *	196
	EPILOGUE	199

* Dagenham posted articles published and/or submitted

Still in my Lynchtime

Dagenham Posted

Its been a few years since I wrote, and published, In My Own Lynchtime – a personal collection of anecdotes about my life, short stories and poems about people and events I have been around for.

Now it is time to look again, for I did not have a lot of room for many of my lifetime experiences, and this time will be a little different. I have sub-titled it Dagenham Posted because many of the personal stories this time relate to my early years in Dagenham/Ilford, and which I have since written for the Dagenham Post. There are also the short stories and a poem or two that never found their way into the previous book, but there is more.

Having reached the celebrated age of 'three score years and ten' (plus 1) I also hold some opinions about the world we live in – most people of my generation do. Since it would be hard to find a more accessible public and personal platform than this one, I am including some of them here. These are 'me' on my soapbox!

In this way I hope my words will reach down the years to my children's children and to theirs, to persuade them of the stupidity of drug abuse for example, and tell them of my views on other relevant topics.

Brian Lynch

So, as last time, I seek to inform, to entertain, and stimulate opinion as much as arouse indignation. I need to tell it how it was, for us in a constantly changing world. A world in which for us as kids, life essentials like mobile phones and computers were the stuff of 'science fiction'. We survived the Luftwaffe and as adults we lived under the threat of nuclear war.

Brian Lynch December 2006

1

Dagenham Posted

Where's ya bin?

For us kids the Battle of Britain, and everything that followed it up to May 1945, was a bit of an adventure – part of our everyday life. We never really appreciated that the sods flying over our shelters each night during the blitz etc were actually trying to kill us.

What I do remember is the marvellous sense of community spirit that kept everyone in the neighbourhood involved with each other. The men – or those that were left behind after others were called up – did their usual day jobs and then spent their nights fire-watching, or roaming the streets looking for lights in windows so they could shout 'put that light out!' Very often they also spent their weekends drilling with broomsticks with one of the local Home Guard platoons.

Dad was a case in point. A London trolleybus driver – a 'reserved occupation' because of the need to ensure public transport kept operating during the war – he also did his fire-watching stint. That meant looking out for the incendiary bombs Jerry was prone to drop as a bit of a side-show, and to show the real bombers following them up where to drop their loads.

He also did his stint in the Home Guard, which became known in later years as Dads Army. The highly successful television sit-com made the Home Guard a bit of a joke of course, but it was one told with respect. Some of those guys really would have tied knives to broomsticks and had a go at killing Nazis, if it had become necessary. Captain Mainwaring and his team may have been comic creations, but they also reflected a very serious determination that Britain would not submit meekly to Hitler and his gang.

So, although it may not have been in a battlefield like Libya, France or Burma, London was still a war zone and driving a bus (even worse a trolleybus) through darkened streets lit only by the reflective glare of the searchlights and blazing buildings would have been pretty hair-raising. Those men, and women clippies, were not even sure how they were going to get home – or indeed what they might find when they got there.

Fire watching, particularly during the Blitz, was very important even in suburbia, where it was bit like Neighbourhood Watch is today. The difference was that the people in the street looking out for each other were out to save lives, not just catch criminals. Nowadays it's burglars – then it was Adolf's Arsonists whose little incendiary bombs (I think they were made from phosphorous) could cause quite a blaze if they happened to fall on someone's house, a factory roof or onto a fractured gas main.

Once located they could be put out fairly easily though, and our house in the Avenue had a porch which we shared with next door and, because of Dad's fire-watching activities, was also where the neighbourhood stirrup pump was kept.

This pump was little more than a brass bicycle pump with a rubber hose attached. You dipped the hose into a bucket of water, pumped like mad and a stream or spray came out of the other end. Very light and portable, they were never likely to put out a small bonfire let alone a blazing house, but they were sufficient to deal with the incendiaries Jerry was happy to lob into our streets on the off chance of setting fire to our spuds and cabbages.

I remember one early evening raid when Mum was on her own in the house, with Dad either at work or out with the firewatchers. She had my young brother Roy and me there though, and had no time to get us down the garden to the shelter before the bombs started whistling down in our direction. We were in the front room and she shoved us both under the dinner table that, while a fairly solid oak job, would not have taken much to become oak splinters.

Very soon it was clear that something was clearly happening outside our house – someone shouted to Mum through the letterbox to go and turn her gas off at the main. While she was out in the scullery doing that, I broke the rules and peeked out through the blackout curtains. A huge sheet of orange and blue flame was roaring up into the sky from the street outside our front gate. Jerry had apparently hit a gas main, and one of his incendiaries had lit the blue touch paper so we were in danger of becoming roasted Lynches.

I don't remember how long it took them to get that blaze under control, but I do know that, although the whole house had been shaken with the explosion outside when the gas had ignited, not one of our windows had so much as a crack in it. Even the tomatoes ripening off on the window frames hadn't moved. Certainly the stirrup pump in the porch would not have done much to save us if the hit had been any closer. Nevertheless I got a good hiding from the old man over it.

You see, it was doing nothing except sit temptingly in the porch all day long so whenever we local urchins got bored and Mum wasn't looking, we would ambush passing pedestrians with it. We had a privet hedge outside our house, just high enough for us to crouch down behind it with a bucket of water and the stirrup pump. We also had the bushes that ran down the centre of our dual carriageway road opposite and which contained 'jungle' hideouts whenever we needed one.

So, as unsuspecting citizens passed by we would leap up either from behind the privet hedge, or from the bushes across the road, and let them have the full pump load.

It was all great fun until Lusher – Police Constable Lusher – spotted us while he was working in his own garden four doors away and warned us off in no uncertain terms. Do you know, over the years we really grew to hate that man who was always spoiling our fun.

By that time the pump was getting very hard to operate anyway, mainly because we were not too fussy where we got the water. Clearly we could not use Mum's scullery without giving the game away – but the bushes just across the road did hold many deep and muddy puddles that were very useful for scooping up bucket refills. In fact we even sometimes even used the puddles themselves without benefit of bucket, to ambush our victims.

Anyway, a few nights after Lusher put a stop to our stirrup-pump bushwhacking, we had the little incident involving our gas main. When Dad's fire-watching pals tried to use the pump while they waited for the fire brigade to come, they got barely a trickle out of it no matter how hard they pumped.

It turned out that the pipe and much of the brass barrel was full of mud. Lusher blew the whistle on us, and I got a bloody good hiding along with a fatherly lecture on sabotaging the war effort.

That, on reflection, was a bit strong coming from him, in view of what happened with the pig bin. These were days when 'Dig for Victory' was the great buzzword and people like us living on the great Becontree Estate were all turning their gardens into mini smallholdings. Most, like ourselves, had come out of East End slums where tiny backyards, potted aspidistras and window-boxes never really provided much of a learning curve for growing rows of spuds, cabbages and runner beans, let alone tomatoes and cucumbers.

So, come the war they were all learning about gardening as they went along, partly because of cost but also to help supplement the ration books. Newspapers carried gardening columns, usually featuring a cartoon character of a grizzled old geyser with a pipe and big hat, explaining the mysteries of double digging and pruning. One of these mysteries centred around the compost heap which of course not only provided good fertilizer, but recycled dinner leavings as well.

Every self-respecting new gardener had his own pile of rotting veg down the end of the garden, adding an extra whiff to the excitement of life in the Andersen Shelter, which was usually sited within smelling distance of that and the chicken run.

These were the 'waste not – want not' years, when kids were forced to eat their greens and being reminded that children in some other countries would have loved to have what we wanted Mum to throw away.

Recognising that not everyone was into composting however, the government had also arranged for galvanised dustbins to be placed at convenient sites in the street. They were the 'pig bins'; into which kids would be sent out to scrape leftover meal scraps off the dinner plates. Then, once a week, the somewhat smelly bins would be emptied into equally smelly trucks, and sent off somewhere to be processed into pigswill, for the nations bacon to get fat on. Or so we were told.

Now, as I said Dad was driving buses throughout the blitz. These were not ordinary diesel buses but trolleybuses whose overhead power lines were particularly vulnerable to enemy action. That often meant bus crews and passengers being stranded in all kinds of strange places at odd hours. It also meant that very often he had to walk home to Dagenham from places as far away as Ilford or even Stratford if he had missed the last bus (or in fact had been driving it himself).

Clearly he was very keen to get home to make sure we were alright. That often involved walking, and bomb dodging, through the raids with the ack ack guns blasting away in all directions. One night not long after our gas main went up, we were having another particularly heavy raid – well we had a lot of them actually.

This particular time Mum had managed to get Roy and I into the shelter along with Granny Lacey, (her mum who lived with us) but clearly she was also very worried about Dad as well. Only rich people had phones then of course and mobile phones were the stuff of science fiction, so it was just a case of sitting in the shelter, listening to the bombs and not knowing where Dad was. We could only pray he was alright – just as he was anxious about us during that raid as well.

In fact he made it back to the Avenue at the height of the raid that night, and was just about to dash indoors when he realised the street was empty, noisy of course, and very dark. By the light of the moon (the bombers loved moonlight of course) and the searchlights, he spotted our local pig bin sitting seductively and lonely in its usual place about thirty yards from our door. He realised he had a golden opportunity while everyone else was in their shelters – one which would give great impetus to his compost heap and do wonders for our garden crops.

Still wearing his busman's uniform he dashed over to the bin and picked it up. By its weight he could tell it was over half full, so in a flash he was up on his toes in the direction of our front gate. All this time the war was going on above and around us of course, but he opened our front door, raced down the passage and through the scullery out into the garden.

Mum heard, rather than saw, him coming. He dashed past the shelter with his ill-gotten gains in his arm to his compost heap, where he emptied the entire contents of the pig-bin. Then, shouting to us that he was fine and would be back in a minute, he rushed back down the garden and into the scullery with the pig bin clutched in his hands in front of him. He was half way down the passage towards the front door when the land mine dropped across the road.

Now these land mines, which floated down on parachutes, were very powerful bombs indeed – in fact this particular one took out four or five houses on a corner almost opposite us and fifty yards down the road. As it exploded it unleashed a tremendous blast capable of taking doors and windows, not to mention roof tiles, out over a wide area. Dad was about half way down our passage with the pig bin in his arms when the blast hit our, still half open, front door. It ripped it from its hinges and sent it hurtling down the passageway straight at him.

Before he knew what was happening he was being blown back down the passage, still clutching the bin in front of him – which probably saved his life – and with his own front door helping him on his way. He finished up on his back by the scullery door beneath both bin and front door.

The ARP and fire-watching chaps – neighbours all – were out and about by then, and had seen our door go in. Some of them dashed in to see if they could help (or more likely see if they could nick anything). They found Dad, dazed and disorientated in a heap on the floor with, what was very clearly the street's galvanised pig bin, and our front door lying on top of him.

This could have been awkward, especially since the bin was

sandwiched between Dad and the door; but the old man, and his Wapping upbringing, was up to it. Even as they helped him to his feet, he was thinking fast. "Look at that", he gasped, "That bloody pig bins only took my door off!"

No one ever apparently asked why the bin was empty.

2

Dagenham Posted

Fiddler on the hoof

We all know Dick Turpin was an Essex vagabond with a predilection for lengthy horse rides and inviting people to hand him over their cash and other valuables. But there was another, more recent, one –and this one had a brother called Randolph who shocked the boxing world in 1951 by beating up an American boxing icon called Sugar Ray Robinson. The brothers Turpin also got hoofed out of Dagenham that year for holding people up for their cash, in a manner of speaking.

It's all gone now, but the big eye-catcher at Becontree Heath was the Merry Fiddlers – a huge rambling pub with a sporting reputation. Behind it was a football pitch used by the pub teams playing in a Sunday morning football league. In the fifties it was also the venue for regular wrestling programmes usually featuring the 'world heavyweight wrestling champion' Bert Assirati.

I have no idea how kosher Bert's claim to being the world champion was, but his name was always writ large on posters stuck to walls in and around Dagenham, long before 'Big Daddy' and 'Giant Haystack' threw their first paddy on TV.

The ring erected regularly for the wrestling, was also used for the occasional boxing tournaments; and it was there that Randy Turpin came with his brother Dick, sometime after he won his

Still In My Own Lynchtime

world middleweight title in 1951 – and shortly before he lost it back to Sugar Ray a few months later.

This was billed as an exhibition match between the Turpin brothers, and not unnaturally it attracted a huge crowd of local boxing fans. That included a bunch of teenagers – the Mild Bunch – who lived not far away in Becontree Avenue.

For Buddy, Ginger and I these were our 'tearaway' years before being torn from Mum's arms to learn how to kill Russians. We were regularly banned from the Ilford Palais, reshaped our toes in winkle-picker shoes and 'flashed the ash' from chromium-plated cigarette cases with built in lighters. The lure of seeing the great Randy Turpin do his stuff in a local pub was always going to be a goer.

So one evening that summer we joined the crowds at the back of the Fiddlers and, glasses of brown ale in hand, excitedly waited to see our first real live British world boxing champion. When he and brother Dick emerged the whole arena went berserk, because the guy really was a British hero who had duffed up a boxing legend. They climbed into the ring to be introduced – Dick was a top-flight boxer in his own right as well – we cheered them to the echo.

They got unrobed, squared up to each other and then went to work (they were both middleweights) – well, of sorts. Yes, admittedly it had been billed as an exhibition match, but it wasn't long before the crowd began to realise that it was being taken for a ride, and it wasn't on the back of a black horse in a northerly direction. These Turpins had no intention of standing to deliver, or of moving around the ring very much either.

This was brotherly love taken too far, with the Turpins just patting each other, laughing, clowning and seemingly totally indifferent to the occasion and what it meant to local boxing fans. They were clearly oblivious to the fact that they were doing so in front of a crowd of Dagenham drunks, who were getting more and more unhappy at what was going on.

Apart from what we'd spent on booze in the Fiddlers, every one there had paid good money to watch some real exhibition boxing with good footwork and genuine world championship skills on display. What we were getting was pantomime punching, comical clinching and Lullaby of Broadway footwork.

Realisation began to seep through ale-befuddled minds that, never mind the Old King Cole panto then on at the London Palladium, this was the night the 'Fiddlers Three' were appearing in Becontree Heath, all merry but only one of them a pub. The other two weren't standing and they certainly weren't delivering – they were having a laugh, and we were the joke.

There wasn't a riot – well, we didn't in those days, did we? But cheers very quickly turned to some quite threatening jeers, and the brothers suddenly realised it was time to get up on their toes – and I do not mean in the boxing sense. They ducked out of the ring, presumably took their money and rode off into the night in their black Jaguars.

At least our Essex Dick Turpin had some class!

3

SOAPBOX

After Beslan

In September 2004 we watched a dreadful sequence of events that followed when a Russian school was invaded by terrorists. The images of terrified children surrounded by bombs, being threatened by hooded gunmen and the stories of them having to drink their own urine, may never leave us.

Journalists, of course, called it a 'slaughter of the innocents', saying thank God it couldn't happen here Really? Who says?

That school was in a town was called Beslan but those small faces etched with fear, were a dreadful reminder of similar pictures taken over half a century earlier, in another hell with a similar name. The children's faces may not have been as skeletal as the young victims of Belsen were, but their eyes showed the same quality of fear and despair.

We live in a world far removed from the one many of us grew up in, and while what happened in 2004 may have taken place in a school far away in Russia, it set new and terrifying frontiers in an ever-shrinking world. Those who carry out such atrocities will always try to justify them with perverted reasoning; but what was really frightening was that Beslan demonstrated just how vulnerable schools are, wherever they are.

It also showed to the terrorists what emotive hostages children make.

Whether of religious, cultural, political or ethnic origin, fundamentalism is boosting international terrorism to unprecedented and merciless levels of savagery that have little compassion where children are concerned. Even in Britain we've seen them killed and maimed by bombs built by 'Christians' and planted to explode indiscriminately in city centres. More recent attacks in London show that, in that sense, little has changed.

Sadly, children make easy and very vulnerable hostages for the fanatics. The more ill equipped such children are in health, social or academic terms, the heavier the emotional blackmail attached to their seizure.

Some years ago, when I was writing the business pages for a local newspaper, I met a Chelmsford businessman – a former SBS Royal Marine paramedic and Gulf War veteran. His company was providing basic first aid courses to schools and other organisations in and around Essex. A survival specialist he was also working with a former SAS man, one of the Bravo Two Zero team out of the first Gulf War, teaching journalists how to survive in hostile environments.

God forbid that there should be any sort of 'Beslan attack' on a British school, but there was one particular aspect that we must learn from the Russian one. It was that the people best able to protect the children from panic (or worse), and give them the strength to survive their ordeal, are the ones who just happened to be in the wrong place at the wrong time.

I grew up sheltering from the Luftwaffe in a shelter surrounded by adults who never showed, at least to us kids, any panic. It is easy to laugh at the British 'stiff upper lip' concept, but it stopped us from being frightened on those terrible nights. Our parents may have been screaming with fear inside, but if so they never passed panic on to us.

Whatever their normal role in the school is, all adults working in them should now be taught how to respond to such a crisis.

Basic first aid should, in any case, be on the national school curriculum and not just to deal with terror. Even just the knowledge of how to bandage a cut finger, deal with a slashed artery or even a heart attack in a superstore, can help children cope with injury to others or themselves without panicking. This must now be part of every child's education; but the really essential people to be taught it are those working with them.

Beslan also showed that it is urgent that they be trained in crisis management. They do not need to be lengthy and complex time-consuming courses – just long enough to learn basic personal survival techniques, and how to prevent panic – perhaps even how to deal with captors.

At least one senior person (perhaps the deputy head) should have the responsibility of ensuring that everyone on the staff – from kitchen cook to site manager as well as teaching staff – has done such a course.

With fundamental terrorism now showing itself in our country, we must not ignore what happened in Russia, casually shrugging our shoulders and assuming it could never happen here. Because it already did!

In March 1996 a lone maniac with guns terrorised a Scottish school in a small town called Dunblane. He shot dead sixteen children and a teacher, leaving many more fighting for their lives in hospital. Ironically, just as in Beslan, much of Thomas Hamilton's murderous activity took place in the school gymnasium.

As a direct result of Hamilton's actions, security in schools now is much tighter than it ever used to be. Not because we want that, but because a single madman had shown it to be necessary. Fundamentalism, and its not always Islamic fundamentalism, already exists, as we have seen in London recently.

For those determined enough, weapons and bombs are easy to acquire, and if we ignore the lessons of Dunblane and Beslan, we fail our children. Politicians, always anxious to make capital out of their own ideas on how education should be organised must not ignore the lessons of a small Russian, and an equally small Scottish, schools.

The LEAs should be pressing for money to fund the crisis training that must now be provided. Enormous resources are being spent educating school governors to be unpaid school managers and on other non-essential projects. This is money that would be better spent educating teachers, cooks, cleaners and caretakers to cope with terrorism.

After Dunblane a parent/governor of the school who found that her daughter had not been among the victims admitted: *'I felt relieved – and then terribly guilty that I felt relieved'*.

I hope the day never comes when another British school governor, councillor, MP or political leader, is forced to express regret and guilt for a similar reason.

4

Becky knows

Having successfully (hmmm) raised four Lynchlings in previous years I thought I was fairly well used to their little ways. Becky, our one and only granddaughter, has been surprising us constantly however, ever since she arrived on the scene, and one such moment will always be with me. She was four years old at the time.

It began when Dearly Beloved expressed the wish that I should pop over to the farm shop to buy her some spuds for Sunday lunch. As an additional delight she suggested that I could take Becky, who had been staying with us overnight, and show her the new lambs that farmer Andrew McTurk had installed in one of his barns that week.

So, spuds safely stowed in the boot, we duly did the *'Ahh Ooh'* bit about the three little woolly creatures clambering all over their mother, before I belted the Beck back into the motor and drove away from the farm. We had not even reached the main road when it started, though she had clearly been deeply in thought as we left the farmyard.

'Granddad. Where to baby lambs come from?'

Now you have a problem. You are not quite sure just how her mother has explained, or indeed whether she has gone into any kind of detail, on this particular topic. I hummed and haa'd for a couple of hundred yards while I thought about it, and finally plumped for: 'They come from their mummy's tummy'.

I really should have known better. This is the child whose

mother had arrived home one day from her own infant school, to announce that it was organising a 'sponsored silence' for charity and she was going in for it. Well, I mean! The entire family – and my late parents happened to be visiting that day – fell about laughing at the very thought of this particular Lynchling shutting up, even for money.

I remember suggesting I wrote to the school asking if I could organise family coach parties so more of the aunts and uncles could witness this unique – one off – event. The child herself though, had been very indignant about the reception her announcement had caused.

'What's so funny about me going in for a sponsored silence', she'd demanded, forcing the gales of laughter to come even louder.

This was the daughter who, when we had travelled on a family holiday to Scotland through the night, was the only one who had stayed awake, happily rabbiting, the entire night as I drove north. With her track record, it is no wonder her daughter has more than a touch of the verbals herself.

All this had flashed through my mind that morning when Becky asked me about the lambs, and I felt pretty pleased with myself that I had successfully sidetracked her. I hadn't. Her response was almost immediate.

'Well, where to baby chicks come from then?' Oh no Beck, – you don't fool me with that one.

'From eggs', I beamed across my shoulder at the tiny blonde babbler in the back seat, thinking I'd cracked it. I should have known better.

'Well, where to eggs come from, then? Now I was starting to panic a bit. All the old memories started to flood back into my mind. Was there no end to this? I fell back onto the old routine.

'From hen's tummies, because hens are chick's mummies'.

That was the reply that really opened the floodgates. I was now bombarded with a torrent of questions about the origins of cows, ducks, elephants, deer, tigers and lions. She was unstoppable as she cross-examined me from the comfort of the back of my own car, about baby animals.

My answers, which had begun quite patiently and amiably,

began to get a little tense and terse as I repeated time and again 'They come from their mummy's tummy!'

I started to remember that night going to Scotland again and how her mother, at about the same age then, had driven me to distraction by asking that if horses ate hay, what did every animal from sharks to snakes... eat. It seemed to go on for mile after tedious mile as I drove in the darkness along the A1. Mile after mile of repetitious questions that began to drain me – and now I was getting the third degree from her daughter, for God's sake.

Becky had been going at it, running down a complete list of zoo and farmyard animals birth routines, from the moment we had left the farm shop. She literally hadn't stopped asking the same damn question, with different species, and getting the same answer each time.

'Where do puppies come from then?' Wearily, almost impatiently but with the winning post in sight so to speak, I repeated by answer about them coming from their mummy's tummy. *'Oh no, they don't!'* she retorted.

Now I have to confess that that gave me a bit of a jolt. To suddenly get an argument instead of her conjuring up yet another four-legged friend to torment me with, caught me off guard. *'Really, Beck. Well, where do puppies come from then?'*

"From pet shops!" – her reply was instant, equally patronising and more than a little scornful.

Which is why I frightened the life out of a blue Mondeo driver by coming within inches of skidding into him as he was legally driving down the road towards me. If he is reading this – I do apologise.

5

STORY

I killed my wife yesterday!

I don't remember ever having been in that particular pub before – in fact South London is not my kind of area at all and I don't think I'd ever even drunk tea there, let alone go into a pub. In fact I can't even remember the name of the damn place, but I was in need of a rest and a quiet pint while I read the morning paper, so I'd just gone into it without thinking.

I think it must have been one of those pubs that stay open all day, because even though it was only half past ten in the morning, it already had one or two customers sipping the odd pint. To be fair I'd lost all track of time by then. It had been a hard night and as well as feeling dog-tired I must have been looking that way too, unshaven and a bit grubby.

The guy serving behind the bar looked up as I approached it, and looked at me enquiringly, but clearly not at my appearance. He was only interested in what I wanted to drink, and he was almost surly about it.

'Pint of John Smiths, please', I answered his unspoken question, after running my eye along his pumps. As he held the glass underneath the tap, I suddenly realised I was a bit hungry as well. 'Got any pies, or anything?' I asked.

Hardly looking up from the beer nearing the top of the glass, he nodded to his right. 'Dahn the end', he grunted, indicating

Still In My Own Lynchtime

one of those big plastic bins, which looked as though they contained a surprisingly varied selection of rolls and pork pies.

As I moved towards them he finished pouring the beer, put it onto the counter and picking up a plate and a pair of plastic forceps, he arrived 'dahn the end', to lift a pie onto the plate. He handed it to me and I proffered a five quid note, which he took to one of those electronic tills. He fed the details of our transaction into it, and after taking some coins from it, came back to where I was standing to plonk them down onto the counter where I was already sipping that smooth cold liquid.

I glanced around the place, spotted an empty table with a few chairs in a far corner, and made my way over to it. Wearily I sat down and took a long pull from the glass. Slicing the pork pie into segments, I smeared some of them with the mustard from the little yellow plastic sachet that had come with it, before spearing one of them into my mouth with the fork and opening the newspaper I'd bought outside.

I never even saw the guy coming over towards me. The first I knew of his presence was when I heard his apologetic little cough, clearly aimed at attracting my attention. I looked up from the paper to see a smallish weedy elderly man whose dark brown suit had certainly seen better days standing in front of me. What hair he did have hung loosely around his neck and ears, and he was as unshaven and scruffy as I was. The difference was that he was clearly used to looking like that, whereas I wasn't.

His faced twitched as he spoke, or rather stammered, and as he did I caught the unmistakeable fragrance of Scotch on his breath. 'Er, excuse me for asking, but you wouldn't have a cigarette you can spare, have you'?

He saw my eyes narrow, and added hurriedly that normally he didn't smoke. 'But I feel in desperate need of one at this moment', he pleaded.

Well, why not? Putting down the beer I was just about to wash some of the pie down with, I reached into my pocket and pulled out a packet of Rothmans. 'Yeah, sure! Don't worry, I know the feeling myself', I reassured him as I held out the open pack for him to take one. 'Here, have a light too' I added flicking my lighter on.

I hadn't actually intended him to sit down and join me, but as he lit the cigarette and drew gratefully on it, he plonked himself onto the chair opposite me. From somewhere he also produced his glass of whisky, and put that down on the table as well, before speaking again.

'I hope you don't mind, but I really do need to sit for a moment or two and enjoy this. You see, I killed my wife yesterday and when I have finished it, and this' indicating the Scotch, 'I am going to turn myself into the police', he said.

Now, to be fair, I've not had that many people scrounge a fag off me in a pub, and then calmly tell me that they have topped their missus. To put it mildly I was a little bit taken aback, as they say in the posh newspapers – the redtops say 'gobsmacked', but it comes to the same thing. Suddenly my own paper lay on the table, forgotten. Even the pangs of hunger I'd been suffering, were failing to break through the wall of shock, which had suddenly been erected around me.

'Sorry?' I said, a little stupidly, inviting him to repeat what he'd said. He stared at me with a kind of absent minded vagueness on his face, as he did so. Nervously almost, he fingered the cigarette and, for the first time I noticed that they were heavily stained with nicotine. This was the man who'd just claimed he'd not been a big smoker, but I let the point drop as I waited for him to continue.

He seemed to suddenly pull himself together with a start, as though he'd come out of a deep sleep, and smiled. It was a strange sort of smile – not warm but not menacing either, yet it conveyed a sad message. 'I'd like to talk about it to be honest. I really am going to the police once I have got the courage', he indicated the glass, 'but it would be nice to tell someone – even a stranger – the real story. If you have got five minutes or so?' he added.

I nodded, still feeling a little numb, but I had also got the hint so I stood up and picked up his glass. Telling him to hang on for a minute while I got the drinks in, I went over to the bar. Mr Surly came up and I asked him for a couple of doubles, which with his usual bonhomie he served before taking my money and going back to watch the TV at the other end of the bar. I was still in

Still In My Own Lynchtime

something of a daze when I got back to my companion and put the glass, and my pack of Rothmans, down on the table in front of him. After taking another sip from the glass, he began his story.

'We weren't married long' he began. 'In fact she was a barmaid in this pub just over three years ago when we started talking. As you can see, it was fairly late in life for me to even think about marriage and I was well set in my ways, but we got on well. She was younger than me, and had been married before but her husband had found someone else and had gone up on his toes', he paused, to take another sip of the whisky.

'I'd won some lottery money, you see. Not a lot, but looking back now I realise it was certainly enough for Brenda to want to get her sticky hands on', his lips parted again in that mirthless self-cynical smile, as he lifted the glass towards them again. Now he really did have my full attention, and I could hardly wait for him to continue.

'Fact is, I suppose the old saying about no fool like an old fool was never truer. Certainly it summed me up. Why any woman, attractive and still in her early thirties, would want an old codger like me is anyone's guess – unless he's got a few bob of course'.

Even at this stage of his story I wasn't sure what to make of my strange companion. Closer examination of that run-down suit did seem to indicate that it had once been quite an expensive one and his hands, though stained, were neat and well kept. I kept quiet as he drained the whisky glass, and stubbed the cigarette out in the ashtray. Clearly he wasn't going anywhere without finishing his story.

'Do you remember that women years ago who said she was going to spend, spend, spend, when her old man had a big pools win? Well I think Brenda must have been her apprentice, because we'd hardly been married a month when she went on a big spending spree. What could have been a nice little nest egg for us, vanished in a year and a half, and the worst thing was that I was daft enough to let her spend it. She was all sweetness and light and, I suppose if the truth be told, I was scared of losing her by then', he said.

He paused significantly, so I got up and refilled the glasses before coming back to the table, now very keen to hear more. He took a sip from the refreshed glass, and looked up again.

'The first I knew the money was gone, was when I started getting nasty letters from the bank, and more from the gas and electricity companies. Then, when she realised her cheques and plastic weren't any good any more, she started getting really nasty. Her previous husband had left her but it didn't stop her comparing him with me – and with him being a bit macho, you can imagine what she was saying about me.' Another pause for breath, and the inevitable mouthful of Bells, and he continued.

As he did, I found I was feeling a great deal of sympathy for him, because I was comparing my own life with his. I knew exactly what he was talking about, because I'd been there too and almost knew instinctively I knew what he was going to say next, and he never let me down.

'Well, I took it for a long time but the more I did, the worse she got. She had a tongue like a viper – a vicious nagging, shouting poisonous viper, and believe me she had a neat turn of phrase. She took it outside the home as well, using every opportunity to make me look small in front of what friends we did have. Privately most of them sympathised with me, because they knew what a real bitch she was.'

Once again I allowed myself a grim smile, because without knowing it he had described my own situation very well. This though was a man who had obviously done something about it, so I waited expectantly as he prepared to come to the important part of his story. First, he drained the glass again and glanced over at me expectantly. Without a word I went back to the bar to ask Mr Surly for some more Scotch – well I needed another one myself as well by then anyway.

When I got back to the table he was busily helping himself to another of my fags, and he looked up gratefully as I put the glasses down onto the table. He took a sip and picked up from where he'd stopped.

'Well the money situation got worse and the only way I could see to resolve it was to let out spare room. That was her idea too, and what she did was move her latest boy friend in, and it was

Still In My Own Lynchtime

me who became the lodger. In my own bloody house!' he added angrily, shaking his head in despair.

He looked at me. 'Would you believe it, he was a chauffeur – just a bloody chauffeur! She always did like big cars and she'd met him when she did some waitressing at some posh wedding or something. He drove a big Mercedes, and I suppose that once she got fed up with using the back seat, installing him as our lodger was a great move on her part.

'Almost from the day he moved in, I think I knew what I was going to have to do. As I lay there, night after night in the next room listening to them, I was making my plans to kill them. To be honest, I think they would have done for me very soon anyway.'

I felt a rim of sweat around my neck as he spoke, and by now I was swigging the whisky almost as fast as he was. I knew he was coming to the point.

'They both liked their booze, you see', using the explanation to take another sip from his own glass. 'I kept a bottle of Scotch in the cupboard and I also knew they would help themselves to it, when they went out in the Merc to a club one night. He never seemed to be too bothered about risking his licence, so I was fairly confident they would help themselves to it.

'I had some sleeping pills that had been prescribed months ago, so I crushed some up and put them into the bottle. Sure enough, as soon as they'd gone I checked the cupboard and the bottle was gone. So I got my things together and followed them down to the club.'

He was almost perky now, but my own heaving tummy had reappeared. I waited for him to tell me, what I was sure he was going to.

'I seemed to wait for hours, parked just a few yards from the Mercedes they were in outside the club, but they didn't notice me. In fact they never even went into the place – just enjoyed my Scotch, and each other, on the back seat. Then the windows started to steam up and it was pretty obvious from the movements of the car, what they were doing.' Another pause, another sip and another puff.

'After about half an hour, all movement inside the car

appeared to stop, and I got out of mine and walked over to peer inside it. I could just make them out – both half naked, but out cold in the back. Whether it was the booze, the tablets or what they had been getting up to, I have no idea. All I knew is that my time had come', he said.

He explained how he'd inserted the rubber hose he taken with him into the car's vent, and had attached it to the exhaust before going back to the driver's seat where the chauffeur had thoughtfully left the keys in the ignition. He'd started the engine, shut the doors and had gone back to his car to watch and wait.

Half an hour later he'd gone back to the Merc. After ascertaining his victims were clearly dead, he'd removed the hose from the exhaust and the car, turned the engine off and driven away. Once again that mirthless smile failed to light up his face, but he was obviously quite happy about what he'd done. He came back to reality with a jerk.

'That was yesterday. I've been walking the streets ever since, trying to come to terms with what I've done because basically I am a very law abiding man. Now I am ready to go and give myself up, so thank you for being such a good and understanding listener', he told me.

He stood up to go, but I held him back. 'Look, let me get you another drink before you go. I think I owe you that,' I told him. Another pilgrimage to the bar, across a pub, which was getting quite full now, to get the glasses refilled again. I came back and we drank them in silence, before he muttered his thanks and threaded his way out into the street again apparently on his way down to the police station.

I sat for a while fondling my own glass for a few minutes, thinking about the story my strange companion had told. Mr Surly had left his position behind the bar to come around the tables clearing up empty glasses and emptying the ashtrays, interrupted me.

'Old Jack been giving you the story of how he killed his missus', he laughed. The look of astonishment on my face must have told its own story, and he chuckled again.

'Do you know, that old sod has got more free drinks out of that story than anyone I know. The truth is that he's been married to his old woman for over thirty years, and she keeps him a bit short of money.' I continued to look stunned. 'Honest, mate, it's true. Just ask any of the regulars in this pub', he added, still laughing as he walked away.

I followed him back to the bar – for now I needed another stiff drink myself. 'Well, I must admit, it was a good story', I told him as I went back to my table, and my cigarettes. I opened my newspaper again and the big black words leapt out at me again, just as they had when I'd been interrupted.

'Man and woman found dead in car park!' The story told how police were treating it as a suspicious death, because someone had turned the engine off after the couple inside had died of carbon monoxide poisoning. The report also said that police were anxious were keen to talk to the woman's husband who they named.

Beneath the headline were the pictures – my wife Brenda, that bloody chauffeur, and me – and in my pocket I fingered the keys to that Mercedes that I should have left in the damned car.

6

All at sea
(From the sublime to the ridiculous)

I spent some of my happiest years at sea, though initially they were only because of the notion by HM Government that I should help defend my country. So it was that I was dragged away at a very early age – well I was 19 actually – from the rainwashed streets of Dagenham to be a sailor.

H M S Raleigh

On December 6th, 1954 I had my first sight of HMS Raleigh – the 'brick battleship' in Torpoint, just a ferry ride from Plymouth. Along with a few dozen other young bucks I saw it from the back of the naval truck which had picked us up at the railway station and which had delivered us into our National Service.

It had been weeks since I'd received the suggestion from Her Majesty's government that I might like to pop along to their Wanstead medical centre, get myself checked out and sit the 'exams' that would determine the general direction of my life for the next couple of years. Having been 'grabbed, groped and coughed' on an medical assembly line of nervous and self-conscious semi-naked teenagers, we had been tested to see if we had any brains at all. Then, somewhat cynically, we were asked for our preferences, as if that made any difference to them.

Most of the lads had said they wanted to do their time in the

RAF – and got the army of course; but some of us had been deemed intelligent enough and/or had had family connections (like a couple of uncles who had also served – including a distant one who hadn't reported back after Jutland), to be of interest to the Admiralty.

I was about to become Stoker Lynch, C/K946568, and spend a couple of years wearing what was still considered to be the best bird-pulling gear on the Ilford Palais dance-floor, and learning how to sink Russian warships at the same time. Just to emphasise their urgent need for my services they also sent a railway travel warrant.

By the time we reached Plymouth that day some of us had got to know each other in the station and train bars. It was all pretty obvious, by our age and suitcases, where we were going even though not all of us were headed for the same uniform. Most were prospective khaki jobs getting off at various points along the line, but a few of us were headed for Plymouth and HMS Raleigh.

Being quick on the uptake – having being proved intelligent and all that – we guessed that the blue truck waiting at the station with the big white letters RN emblazoned on its doors, had something to do with us. Just in case we hadn't, there was also a rather loud chap, wearing a peaked cap and dark suit with brass buttons, to help us. Brandishing a clipboard in his hand he was inviting us, in some quite noisy and impolite language, to climb up into the back rather quickly.

We all clambered aboard, after chucking our suitcases (which we had been told to bring so we could send our civvies home) onto it and, I suppose to add to the mystery of the tour, the end flap was closed behind us. We were all still making silly nervous jokes about only two years to demob etc, when our 'chauffeur' began hurling his truck through the back streets of Plymouth (Devon) in the general direction of what was presumably Torpoint (Cornwall).

Eventually it stopped, the back flap was ripped open and there was Petty Officer Loudmouth again – still being very offensive – shouting and hollering at us to get down and line up in front of the guardroom. Clearly it was best to humour him, and most of us almost fell out of the truck.

We found ourselves just inside the gates of HMS Raleigh, in front of a guardroom which had two rather attractive little cannons decoratively placed on each side, and a flagpole, which was flying the white ensign not far away. We would soon learn to salute these guns whenever we passed them either on our way into our out of the base.

P.O. Loudmouth, having gained our attention and got us into some kind of order, now noisily explained that he would be our mother and father for the next few months – implying that he himself had not had such benefits, presumably having been born out of wedlock.

Clearly he was already having a bad hair day, and having met us wasn't in the best of moods. He prowled up and down our ragged lines, stopping here and there to make some sarcastic remark at one or another of us. We were all dreading him stopping in front of us and, inevitably, he stopped in front of me.

"Wherejewcomefrom?" he bawled in my face. I stammered that I was from London, and that seemed to make him even more uptight.

"Wot you doin' ere, then? Wot do you know about ships and the sea dahn there in the Smoke? At least some of these others come from sea towns", he snarled. Now in the course of the next few months we learned a great deal, and one of those things was to keep schtumm when faced with such questions. Me, I had to go and reply.

"Been to Ramsgate on me 'olidays, sir". I mumbled – I thought he was going to have a fit.

"Sir? Sir?" he shrieked, "Listen you lot – I ain't a bloody 'Sir'. I am your worst nightmare, a cow-son, a 'shit' of the first order. I am a Petty Officer. You do not salute me – and you do not call me, bloody sir, but you do whatever I bloody well tell you to do. Is that clear?" he screamed the last few words, but at least he was screaming them to all of us, and no longer homing in on yours truly.

That was only the start. For the next few weeks – they actually sent us home on leave in uniform (bless 'em) for Christmas – PO

Loudmouth was true to his word, as he worked hard making our lives a total misery. He marched us in the snow from dawn to dusk, with and without battered old wartime rifles, teaching us the rudiments of 'drill', in slow time, normal and – more often than not – on the double. Having supervised the issue of our kit, he insisted on having it all laid out in proper order every day. He had us swilling out the toilets (heads) before lights out, and sent us to the barbers so many times a week he must have been copping more backhanders than Tim Henman.

There were others also involved in making our stay in Torpoint memorable. The dentist was one. In those days I grew my own teeth although, having been turned off dentists by the experiences of the 'school dentist', they were not in the best of condition.

The Navy clearly felt we should all have good teeth and thus we all had the usual 'open wide' inspections as soon as we arrived. All seemed well until one day, PO Loudmouth called me out of parade and told me to report to the dentist who, having perused the results of my medical, had expressed a desire to see me. I was not best pleased at this.

In fact by the time I got to the dentist surgery I was pretty wound up about the whole thing. I walked in and (me and my big mouth again) demanded to know of the dentist why he wanted me. In hindsight I do not believe that I couched this request in the most appropriate way. He went spare!

He was, as he explained at length, an officer and one did not speak to officers in the way I had. He shouted at me and told me to sit in his chair. The gist of his speech from then on was that it was my duty to just do as I was told and not to question officers' motives. I had a filling which needed doing and that is what I was going to get.

I have to admit he did a good job on the filling – it lasted for many years. My only regret at the time though was that, had I been a bit more respectful towards an officer, he might have given me something to deaden the pain, instead of using cold steel to practise his arts on my dodgy molar.

Which is why, whenever I see the word Raleigh my mind goes

back to that day, that poor fatherless Petty Officer Loudmouth and a vicious dentist.

Serving on the Gay Boats

Every ex national serviceman says it never did him any harm, but while he was doing it he wasn't usually in the same frame of mind. Many of the lads my age saw active service in the army and RAF in places they probably had never heard of a few years before their call-up. Some of them were killed or maimed in the jungles of Malaya or in places like Cyprus, Kenya and we should not forget Korea. In fact my brother, Roy, did his time in the army in Cyprus though, fortunately, without coming to harm.

So I was lucky – and in several ways. I fell into a job in the navy that many would have given their eyeteeth for – I became part of a 'ferry crew', though this was nothing like the Woolwich Free Ferry.

After we got back from our Christmas leave, we had all the prospect of finishing our basic training learning to be 'stokers' at HMS Raleigh, but they asked for volunteers for a special course on internal combustion engines. The attraction was that this was done on an old Cunard liner moored up the river from Devonport, so we could leave Raleigh behind us. We all volunteered and three of us – Lenny Broadhurst from Colchester (nicknamed 'Swede' of course), Harry Willard, who was older than us because he'd done his training as an architect, and myself – were accepted.

The Alaunia was little more than a big empty shell containing living accommodation for those on the course. She was tied up alongside an old French destroyer called Dunquerque, and a flat bottom gun monitor, which housed the classrooms, and the NAAFI bar.

For the first time we were living and working with real trained sailors – some of them with considerable sea time in fact. We slept in hammocks (learning not to tie them up for sleeping with a bow that could be pulled apart by some drunken reveller coming back inboard while we slept in them), and we experienced real shipboard living and catering.

I also fell into a dream job without even asking. One of the crew of the Captain's Motor Boat had failed to come back from leave because he was sick and for some obscure reason I was allocated to it. Of course it meant lounging around the messdeck most of the day waiting for the call for the Captain's Motor Boat crew to man their boat, but someone had to do it.

We national servicemen in fact came top of the class when we finished our exams and were deemed fit to operate real diesel and petrol engines. That was when I found out that the ones who came lower down the list were drafted to aircraft carriers and the like, while those like us were sent to either Coastal Forces (Motor Torpedo Boats) or submarines. Now, to be honest, submarines was about the last place I wanted to be, so I was quite relieved when Lenny, Harry and I all got drafted to HMS Hornet in Gosport to serve in the MTB squadrons.

We found we were part of the Sixth Ferry Crew – a team which travelled to different shipbuilders throughout the UK to pick up new MTBs, bring them back to Gosport, work them up by doing their trials and then hand them over to the squadrons while we went and picked up another boat. A brilliant little number, and no mistake, though there was one little drawback, not obvious at the time.

There was a class of Motor Torpedo Boats (MTBs) that they called the 'Gay' boats because they had names like Gay Bombardier, Gay Charger and the like. These were, of course, in the days before the word was hijacked to mean something entirely other than happy, but it is a fact that for some time I walked around Portsmouth with the words Gay Cavalier emblazoned across my cap.

All in all though, HMS Hornet proved to be a pretty good draft compared to what it could have been and although the only foreign place we ever visited in my Royal Navy time was Caen in France, we did see a lot of British pubs.

The French thing is worth mentioning because we were there to mark the tenth anniversary of the Normandy landings at Arromanche, near Caen. We were assured we were popular there because it had been the British who had liberated Caen, but they forgot to tell us that the RAF flattened the place so we were not all God's chosen creatures with everyone there.

We went there with a submarine which was ordered home after three days because its drunken crew went berserk in Caen, and had to be brought back almost en masse by the local French police one night.

Perhaps it is time here to cut to the chase and remember my last couple of weeks in another pre-published piece, when I spent my 21st birthday in a coalhole and finished up as 'Engineer Mechanic Harrison'.

Thank God for Engineer Mechanic Harrison

Some moments stick in your mind for ever, and when Dearly Beloved and I popped into the old Chatham Dockyard one Easter a few years ago, the time where I found myself staring up at an enraged naval officer, pointing my own rifle at me, came back with crystal clarity.

In fact, had it not been for 'Engineer Mechanic Harrison', instead of celebrating the end of my two years National Service I could have served an extended version by spending an uncomfortable Christmas, in an RN prison.

Most of my service had been spent swanning up and down the coast in MTBs, such as the unforgettable Gay Cavalier, but it was cold sweats all round when the Suez war started in the Autumn of 1956, weeks before I was due to be released into the civilian world again. Suddenly the Suez Canal had two armies – one Jewish and the other Egyptian – on each bank, and the possibility of racing up and down between them on tanks of high octane, did not appeal.

However, it all blew over and Harry, Lenny and I arrived back in Chatham's HMS Pembroke, to be demobbed within the fortnight. That was due on the day after my 21st birthday, which in those days was the 'key of the door' day when you officially became an adult and could even vote.

Now anyone who did their bit in the Navy knows that you

can't just walk out of the gates like that – you have to be 'booked out' of a dozen different departments. So they issue you with a 'draft chit', which is a kind of 'skivers' licence that lets you spend days strolling round getting yourself rubber stamped out of service life. While we waited for that magic piece of paper however, we were press ganged into Pembroke's workforce.

This was in November – I was due to be unleashed back into the Palais circuit on my birthday on the 22nd – and it was pretty nippy weather wise. So seeing my name listed for a boiler house working party seemed like a bit of a result. Although we were called Engineer Mechanics by then we were still seen as 'Stokers' by some. Even so, we were all a bit surprised when we reported, to be handed shovels before being marched off to the boiler house. In fact the only coke we would be shovelling was outside in the very fresh air, rather than inside a nice warm place. To this day I can hardly believe what happened.

Chatham barracks was full of little boiler houses, but not all of them had piles of coke to burn – in fact many of them were not even operational. We were marched to one that wasn't working and ordered to bag the pile of coke that lay outside it. Naturally that took us most of the day. Well, little diversions like lunch and the rum issue took up some of the time, but we were in no hurry anyway. We packed the sacks we had filled with coke onto a barrow and were directed to lug it round to another boiler house at the other end of the barracks. There we emptied them all out into a pile again, and marched off for an evening's revelry in a Chatham boozer, happy we had done a good days work.

The next morning we were all marched back to the pile we had created the previous evening – and ordered to bag it all up again to take it to another boiler house. That was the pattern – believe it or not, for ten days we shifted the same pile of coke around Chatham, often to the same space we had emptied it from a couple of days before. It seemed a bit pointless even then, but we were getting closer and closer to 'the day' and that was the important thing anyway.

Now, Dagenham is within easy reach of Chatham by train (at least it was then when we had a proper train service) so I did have the opportunity to nip home for the weekend. With the double celebration of my 21st and demob coming up, I was rather looking forward to my last weekend. Well, I was until I found that, on my birthday and my last Sunday as a sailor, I had been rostered for guard duty. No one would swap duties so I resigned myself to having a few bevvies in the NAAFI with mates, before going on that guard duty watch on that Sunday night.

In fact, by the time we were due to go on watch at 10pm we had swallowed a fair amount of celebratory ale. We were not stoned out of our brains, but it would be fair to say we were 'gibbering' a bit as we put on the official belt and gaiters before lining up to be issued with our rifles.

There was no real security problem in those days – it was years before the IRA etc got serious. The Officer of the Watch, who then went off to his bottle of wardroom gin, leaving the Leading Seaman in charge of the guard that night to organise us, inspected us. One man on watch at a time – the rest could kip on the bare mattresses in an empty barrack room handily close by. We drew lots for an hour apiece – I drew the 1am to 2am slot and we all turned in, each of us having made a note of where the guy we had to wake up was sleeping.

I was duly shaken awake at five to one, and started my lonely vigil. All we had to do was take a turn or two around the parade ground and admin buildings area. There was none of this nonsense about guarding the gate or anything. It was very quiet in the early hours and nothing stirred but, bearing in mind the amount of birthday booze I had sunk a few hours before, I was not at my brightest anyway. After a turn or two around the parade ground I had to sit down and have a smoke, on one of the benches around it. God, I was tired!

Next thing I know, I am getting jabbed ferociously in the shoulder. Through my befuddled consciousness I could hear shouting, some of it appearing to question the legitimacy of my parentage. Blearily I became aware that the hollering was coming from a Lieutenant Commander who was poking me with my own rifle to emphasise his point. What was worse was that behind him lurked a smirking female of the civilian variety, who was clearly enjoying her bloke's macho performance.

Thankfully this guy was not the Officer of the Watch – he was probably back from a heavy night in Chatham, bringing the girl friend back for, er company. He never had the list of overnight sentries with names, but he was going potty anyway. Shrieking threats about Captain's Reports, he was demanding to know my name and number It was at this point that Engineer Mechanic Harrison rode to the rescue in my imagination.

I staggered to my feet and hauled myself up to attention, saluted and glibly reeled off his name and equally fictitious number – details that he actually wrote down. Then he read me my fortune, thrust my rifle back at me and ordered me to report to the Master at Arms by noon. Then he swayed off with girl friend clinging to his arm towards the officer's quarters and presumably a night of lust. I didn't have the heart to tell him I was planning to be in Dagenham by noon.

But I had another little problem. I looked at my watch, and saw it was 4.20am – I had not only done two other people's watches, I didn't know who to wake for the 4am slot. I did know who was on the 5am start, so I had to stay on guard, and make sure I stayed away, until then.

The only way I managed to stay awake was by making sure I was walking, and walking, and walking all around that bloody parade ground in the early hours of that morning. Well, I had plenty to think about anyway, given that I had not only been caught sleeping on watch, I had lied to my back teeth as well. Eventually I staggered back to the dormitory and located the 5am man. I woke him and just fell onto my own bunk again

Only a couple of hours later we were noisily woken up, lined up for inspection and dismissed. No one questioned why they had slept through their watch, and not a word about reports was said by the Officer of the Watch. So far so good.

We were due to leave the place by 10.30am, so for the next few hours I was sweating a little bit. The final touch of irony was when we went to collect our travel warrants and the Navy made its last despairing efforts to get us to stay.

"Have you thought about signing on?"

"Yes sir!"
"You have? And what do you think about it?"
"No chance."
"Right", his friendly tone changed, "Here's your travel permit, good-bye!"

We, and there was four of us involved, could hardly get out of his office quick enough – but I had my own reasons for getting out as well. All morning, right up to the time we were handed that warrant, and we were walking out of the barracks gate laden down with kitbag and all the other gear, I kept getting this nasty feeling I was about to hear an announcement over the public address system, inviting Engineer Mechanic Harrison to report to the Master at Arms.

It never was, and I was not going to hang about waiting for it, but I often wondered if a warrant was ever issued for Engineer Mechanic Harrison C/K...whatever his number was.

Back in Civvy Street, my national duty done, I was at a bit of a loss what to do. I still had cravings for a career at sea, though not with the Royal Navy, but could see no practical way of achieving it. So I went back to the Globe Pneumatic while I was thinking things over. It didn't take long (George White didn't exactly welcome me with open arms) and within weeks I was really on my way back to sea again.

There was once a barmaid called Nell!

Within a few weeks of leaving Engineer Mechanic Lynch C/K946568 behind me in Chatham Barracks, and having convinced a City shipping company that I was too good an opportunity to pass up, Merchant Navy Uncertificated Junior Engineer Officer Lynch was chugging across the Pacific and living it up in the good ship SS Southern Prince.

For the shipping company, the object of the voyage was to drop off a cargo of whisky, iron and cars in New Zealand, and then pop over to Australia for a few thousand bales of wool. In the event Oz managed without us, and we sailed round the coast of the Kiwis picking up the wool from its ports instead. (As it happened these bales of wool caused me quite a problem before we got them home because, thanks to our holds being crammed to the top with the stuff, I actually had a bad bout of hay fever, which, considering we were smack in the middle of the Pacific, was a bit strong.)

Having fled the Navy in December, I'd gone back to work in the Globe Pneumatic Engineering Company. This was not a proposition that met with anything but reluctance on the Globe's part because to be frank, I had not been one of the greatest of their apprentices in the first place. But, because I had been there before being wrenched from my mum's arms to serve my country, they had to employ me anyway.

The firm had moved from Chadwell Heath to Harold Wood by then – at that time almost out in the countryside and with public transport not too clever. (These days I often have to take herself to B&Q, which is a few yards from where the Globe, which later became Fenners was sited.)

I didn't like it then, any more than I had a couple of years earlier. Although I was working for them as a lathe turner, earning quite good cash as it happens, I was looking for a way out before the end of my first tea break. It came when another of the former apprentices mentioned that he had done a trip with the Merchant Navy while I had been away.

He explained how it worked, enthused another one of the lads – Dennis Tibbett – as well as me, and before you could say 'can I have a day off please, guvnor' Dennis and I were in London's Leadenhall Street, where all the big shipping companies were. We did some swift talking, and flashed apprenticeship articles and our national service records. Dennis had been army but in my case the discharge record also contained a 'VG Superior' a kind of commendation given because of the cool way I had reacted during one emergency on the MTBs.

Well to cut a long story short, we were very soon in and booked for a berth in the MV (Motor Vessel) Southern Prince as Junior Engineer Officers, ready to live the life of Riley, being waited on hand and foot by stewards and with ready access to prolific amounts of booze.

This did not please my mother. Having only just returned to the fold after a couple of years away, she was nurturing hopes that it would be settling-down time for her eldest. "People will think you can't get away from us quick enough" she almost cried as she tried to persuade me to change my mind.

Dennis and I joined the ship in Hull in January, just before she sailed to Ostend on a quick visit before coming back to the UK and up the Thames to the Victoria Docks. Apart from the reminder in the Channel that my stomach and I did not exactly agree on our enthusiasm on the sea, all was well so far.

A few days in London – swaggering about at home yapping on about our ship – and we were off to Liverpool to spend three weeks refitting, and taking on our cargo.

I must admit I did like Liverpool. We had some great times ashore in the local pubs there and your average scouser really does have a great sense of humour. Thinking about it, I was in Liverpool in 1957 when the Cavern was at its best, and when young Paul, John and the others were playing church socials round the corner doing their Quarrymen bit.

We eventually sailed out of Liverpool straight into one of the worst storms the Irish Sea had seen in years, and for the next five days and nights, as we headed out into the Atlantic, I was back to my old bucket-carrying engine room routines. It was a pretty bad experience I would prefer not to dwell on. I do remember one grisly night, coming off watch and taking a glass of Andrews Liver Salts in the hope it would calm me down a bit – it was still fizzing as it came back again.

Then one day, my stomach stopped rocking round the clock and began to calm down a little. At last I began to enjoy things as we left the wintry north Atlantic further and further behind us and headed south towards the Caribbean, Panama and the canal.

First we had to bunker (take on oil) in Curacao at one of the huge oil terminals there. I remember a bright and sunny day, with another ship – a gleaming white passenger job – doing the same thing on the other side of the terminal. Now this oil is not your average diesel – it is thick black gungy stuff, which has to be heated and treated before it can actually be used in the boilers.

Suddenly one of the oil pump lines on the smart white liner snapped and began acting like a berserk hosepipe. Within seconds that gleaming white vessel was dripping black as the oil line sprayed it liberally with the oil it should have been pumping into its fuel tanks. Oh dear me, did we have a good old laugh from the decks of the Southern Prince?

I will never forget my first experience of the Panama Canal, a day or so later. The ship is pulled through parts of it by 'mechanical donkeys', and we sat there on deck supping large gin and tonics, and eating crayfish salads as we watched the huge machines do our work. Then we motored gently under our own power through the jungle parts of the canal. I really did see crocodiles crawling down the bank into the water and saw brightly coloured birds sitting on the branches as we passed through. It was hot and steamy day, and the freezing cold of Dagenham – not to mention the miserable atmosphere of the Globe Pneumatic – seemed a long way away.

We spent about five or six weeks in the Pacific after that, usually without another ship in sight – though occasionally at night a brightly lit passenger ship would pass by on the horizon. At night we sailed beneath a cloudless ceiling of unfamiliar stars, watching the phosphorescence in the water and the flying fish skidding along the surface – sometimes being bounced up onto our decks.

It was a marvellous time. There I was, a former ragamuffin from the streets of Dagenham, and only a few weeks after being a Royal Navy 'stoker'. Now I was a ship's officer, giving orders to 'stokers' and 'donkey greasers' down below on watch while picking their brains, and spending our time off watch swigging duty free gin, whisky and crates of cold beer as we crossed the International Date Line. (We had two Wednesdays one week on the outward trip, and one week we had none on the way back.)

Then one day we arrived in New Zealand. I loved NZ. As the Prince cruised gently up the bay into an Auckland bathed in the warm sunlight of a February morning, we caught glimpses of this new (to some of us) and exciting world ashore and beyond the dock gates. We would be cruising around the North and South islands of this land of the Maoris for the next few months, and life was looking real sweet.

Even as we tied up and closed the engine room down dockies, as they always did, were already swarming aboard keen to do some private business before the local Customs arrived and spoiled everything. They were brash, loud and loaded with NZ quids – and that was when the penny dropped with us younger seadogs. We hadn't been able to buy any duty free booze on board for a fortnight – clearly because the Chief Mate and Second Engineer had stocked up in advance. They did some good business that morning.

To us late1950s New Zealand was amazing. In the weeks we were there we swam off its beaches, chatted up some pretty gorgeous Kiwi-birds (unfeathered sort), fished with the local kids for tuna off our decks, and set out to hitch-hike to the famous hot springs of Rotarua – failing miserably because of the difficulties we experienced in getting past the pub at the end of the jetty. Then there was the famous Five'o-clock Swill.

They tell me things have changed a great deal now and that in both NZ and Oz they keep more civilised drinking hours these days. Back then, the pubs shut at 6pm on the dot – just sixty minutes after the normal working day ended at 5pm. Clearly that did not leave a great deal of time for after-work jollies for the drinking classes down under.

We were ok; we kept ship's hours not dockies hours, but we'd had a thirsty trip (especially during the last two weeks) and when Fourth Engineer Duncan McMasters, who'd already done one trip on the ship, suggested we popped out for a beer or three in the nearest pub about four o'clock on that first day, we were easily swayed.

This pub was in clear view, about two hundred yards from the dock gates and by any standards was fairly basic. Not the 'spit and sawdust' jobs we were used to outside British dock gates, but well scrubbed tables and solid wooden chairs – no carpet, a long highly polished bar totally uncluttered by the usual sort of bar furniture, like ashtrays, beer mats or cloths. Standing behind this bar, I swear to God, there was a barmaid called Nell.

Still In My Own Lynchtime

When we boiler-suited Limeys walked in, Nell was already standing ready with a long half-inch rubber tube in hand. In front of her, the bar was covered with small half-pint sized glasses – dozens and dozens of them. We ordered four beers and she used the tube, which had a kind of clamp on it, to squirt beer into four glasses for us, charging us sixpence a glass.

It seemed a bit odd because we were the only ones in the pub yet all these glasses were laid out like it was party time in a Portsmouth NAAFI before a big ship sailed. McMasters, having been there before, smiled knowingly and indicated to us to sit down.

The clocked ticked on and we bought a few more beers. It wasn't the greatest beer on earth – to be honest, it was lousy and tasted of acorns. We knew that after 6 o'clock we would have to go back to the ship to find a decent drink anyway, so by quarter to five we'd already had a few tanners worth of the acorn stuff. Nell, by then, was clearly getting ready for something because she had started to squirt beer into glasses that no one had ordered.

Suddenly we became aware that out of the window a few hundred yards away something was happening. The dock gates were wide open, but although there was clearly a crowd there, no one was coming out of them though we could see them all keep glancing at their watches. McMasters hurriedly got a double round in for us and, at 5pm, a hooter, apparently signalling the end of the day's work, blared out. What followed has remained with me ever since.

It was like the start of a frenzied London Marathon – but these runners were not all on foot. They dashed through those gates on bikes or motor bikes – even a car or two was roaring through those dock gates even before the hooter had come to the end of its wailing.

The shrewder boozers had positioned themselves in the right strategic spot, not so much for a quick getaway, but to make sure that when they reached the finish line they were in front of a convenient door. Their destination was our pub, and we sat there open-mouthed watching through the window as this torrent of human thirst – a floodtide of desperate dockies – came rushing towards us.

They were running and leaping, jumping and swerving in and out on their bikes and motorbikes – how nobody got mown down in the crush I will never know. Even as the first notes of the hooter reached us Nell had upped her speed, and was squirting away like a galvanised human stirrup pump. Within seconds the pub doors had burst open, and the Swill was under way.

Sixpences rained down onto the bar as eager hands grabbed and spilled beer everywhere. What had been a quiet and almost empty pub was suddenly packed and heaving, as more and more dockies forced their way to the front shouting, cussing, yelling, demanding. In front of if all stood Nell, calm and impassive in the pandemonium, scooping up tanners and squirting that lousy beer into empty glasses, filling, refilling and rerefilling as fast as it was disappearing down throats.

The lads had just one hour's drinking time a day – and clearly it wasn't ever wasted in small talk. This was the famous Five o'clock Swill at its cutting, or rather drinking, edge. This was serious boozing. We 'hard drinking' young Brits learned a lot that day – like make sure that in future we had an hour's worth of beer in front of us before the clock struck 5 and not just a double round.

I have seen some drinking in my day – have even occasionally been party to some of it – but I have never before, or since, seen anything like the Swill. An hour later these blokes were falling all over the place, happily stoned out of their brains on that acorn brew, as Nell threw them out so she could close up.

As Winston Churchill, himself something of a toper and bit of an authority on Finest Hours, might have said: "Never before, in the field of human dehydration, was so much downed so fast, by so many".

The Fort Avalon

I have never written a great deal about the Fort Avalon, and I don't really know why because I have always considered it to be the finest year of my young life. Years later I even harboured the idea of going back to her, but it turned out she'd been long sold and renamed.

This was a love affair that began one fine day in 1957, when a New York yellow cab deposited my new Chief Engineer (I seem to remember his name was Jordan) and me onto the dockside of Bush Terminal in Brooklyn, where she'd tied up only half an hour earlier. Jordan and I had been put up in the Times Square Hotel for a few days, after I'd left the Il de France where I'd been a passenger, because the Avalon been late coming in. I'd had a great couple of days rubbernecking in the Big Apple living it up on a few dollars a day expenses, and eating out in some great restaurants, and meeting Jordan for the first time.

First impressions of a ship are always sketchy, because although this one was only 3.500 tons, as against my previous ship the 8,000-ton Southern Prince, from the jetty she looked just as huge. We struggled with our gear up the gangway onto the deck where we were met by the Chief Engineer who was leaving and who took Jordan off to his office.

The Second Engineer was a Geordie called Bill Thomas and he took charge of me, showed me into the 'Engineers Alley' where he introduced me to the Third, Fourth and Fifth engineers – another Geordie, a Scot and a Hampshire man. I was to be the Junior Engineer for one trip, after which I would be the Fifth Engineer replacing the one leaving the ship when it got back to New York. When he did, we were joined by a Scouser, so the UK ports were pretty well represented.

The Fort Avalon was a trader that sometimes carried a couple of passengers. Its usual trip after leaving New York was to St John (Maine) then Halifax (Nova Scotia) before going on to St John's in Newfoundland to unload the rest of whatever cargo we carried. Then we'd go to another Newfoundland port called Corner Brook where the great lumber mills had turned trees into newsprint – great rolls of it which was carried back to New York.

Occasionally the route varied – two or three times we went down to Bermuda and one to a 'one horse' town called Port Union in Newfoundland, where we successfully managed to pull down a brand new jetty because someone was slow in cutting the forward lines as we steamed away.

A steamship she was driven by a turbine engine, powered by steam produced in a couple of big oil fed boilers. That was our domain of course, but I will never forget the first words spoken to me by my new shipmates. 'Do you drink?'

I assured them that I had been known to quaff the odd beer or three and they tossed over a large holdall. They were still wearing overalls, having just closed down the engine room of course, and they told me there was no beer left in the ship. They threw some money together between them and asked me to go down to the end of the jetty where there was a 'dockies' canteen and fill the bag up.

I was young, fit and fairly strong, but by the time the bag had been filled with enough bottles of Budweiser to cope with the money I'd brought, I could hardly lift it. But I managed it and by the time I got back aboard they were cleaned up and ready for a drink. Within the hour I was smashed out of my brain and we were all best buddies.

So much so that I agreed to go ashore into Manhattan with them to visit the Merchant Navy Officers Club, where more booze passed our lips and by which time we'd all become instant shipmates.

A Yellow Cab back to Bush Terminal which we reached to find that the Fort Avalon was being moved along the dock a hundred yards, so we had to wait a few minutes before we could get back aboard. By the time the gangway was in place I was completely legless and my new skipper, Captain Baxter-Powell watched from the bridge as his newest officer was carried feet first back on board.

At breakfast in the officers saloon the next morning I was formally introduced to BP, who made it quite clear that he expected standards from his officers, even engineering officers, higher than he'd witnessed the previous night.

It was time to get down to some serious work though and, although a lot of shore based maintenance work was going on around us, I was introduced to my duties. I would be working the 4-8 watches (4am-8am, 4pm-8pm) with Bill Thomas, the Second

Still In My Own Lynchtime

Engineer, doing mostly routine work but also testing the boiler water every day for its alkaline and acid levels. The engine itself was a huge (to me) steam turbine job, which I would eventually be shown how to drive, though my first job when preparing for sea was to go aft and check the steering gear.

A couple of days later we were cargoed up and ready for sea – I was quite happy and looking forward to it all, but there was a problem. The seamen on board (mainly Newfoundlanders) had gone on strike, and it took hours before that was all settled and we headed out of the Hudson en route to the Atlantic and Maine, where St John was our first and usual port of call.

One happy result was that the Fort Avalon was the first, and only, ship I was never seasick on, but by God she was a hard drinking ship, and it turned out that that first day had been just about par for the course. Apart from Bill Thomas I cannot remember all their names now, but they were the best bunch of blokes I ever sailed with and all contributed to the 'work hard play hard' ideal. The engineer's alleyway always had a party going on with bottles of gin or packs (24) of Budweisers flowing freely

We went to Bermuda a couple of times, and on one occasion after we left, we all celebrated with 90pcnt proof Bermuda rum in the Second's cabin. Great, until 4am when it was time to get up for the watch – I made it down there alright but Bill didn't appear.

Throughout the watch I kept sending a stoker up to shake him but he couldn't be shaken and although I was doing the job I wasn't technically qualified to do it. I even 'blew the funnels' – an exercise which involved blasting all the soot out of the funnels to clean them, and for which the ship had to alter course so she was sailing into the wind. I did all that without the bridge realising they had a complete duffer in the engine room, and it wasn't until 7.15 that we finally managed to wake the Second engineer.

We sailed the Avalon through all kinds of weather – a back end of a hurricane when the entire stern was being lifted out of the water and we had to quickly shut the steam down until she settle back in again. If we'd left the steam on, the screw would have spun so fast it could have come apart – so it was quite a dangerous time. On other occasions in the winter off the coast of Newfoundland, big chunks of pack ice would thud into the side of the ship, sometimes giving the nasty feeling we were about to have a Titanic moment.

Perhaps one of the worst was when we had an engine failure one day, and it was a case of all hands down into the engine room. The ship lost power of course and was drifting so much there was talk of calling the local coastguard out for help. We kept getting phone calls in the engine room asking for progress, and Jordan kept shouting back at them to give us a chance.

Finally, we sorted the problem and reported we could get under way again. There was an immediate demand for reverse engines followed by another ring on the telegraph to resume normal speeds. I went up on deck for a breather and almost collapsed – we had been yards from some of the most vicious rocks outside Cornwall. Baxter-Powell, presumably keen to ensure there was no salvage issue involved, had taken a gamble on us getting the ship going again.

I have written a separate piece about New York, which as the Avalon's home port and the start of each of the monthly voyages we made. I loved New York, and its people, but I suppose the place that made the biggest impression on me was Bermuda. We visited the place twice and, apart from going through the Panama Canal in the Southern Prince, this was the nearest I had been to the West Indies, or at least the Caribbean.

The pink sands, wonderful climate and the old town of Hamilton, where I bought my first Brownie cine-camera. We could hire small motorbikes, mopeds really, and ride up into the hinterland of the island to visit a pub called the Smugglers Inn, where we drank their 'swizzles', which resulted in a few problems actually riding back to Hamilton. There we would buy the 90pcnt proof rum that mixed so well with the coca cola that I had the experience of being unable to get the second engineer down on his watch one morning.

It was also in Bermuda that we tied up alongside one of Furness Withy's other ships – the Queen of Bermuda, which had just lost one of its stewards. His stage name was Tommy Steele, and by then he was making it big back home as our first real rock and roller.

It was a year I remember most of all for Bermuda, but it was all going to turn sour not long after our second visit there – which was also when we ran into the back end of a hurricane that could have caused us so many problems. Whether it was the strain of that, or other personal problems he had I don't know but on the way back to New York our chief engineer (Jordan, who I'd joined the ship with) had a bit of a nervous breakdown and had to be taken off when we got back to the Big Apple.

For one trip Bill Thomas, our second, was made up to chief engineer and we all got moved up a slot. In my case that meant being the fourth for while, handling my own watch (8-12) and being in charge of the refrigeration unit. I knew next to nothing about refrigeration, but it did mean I had a key to the cold room and as a result we had some great lobster sandwiches in the engineers alley that trip. That upset Baxter Powell because they were his personal stock of Maine lobsters and he actually held an enquiry to establish why some were missing.

I was the first under suspicion of course (I had the key), but I acted so indignantly over the allegation that he hurriedly apologised to me and said it was probably down to the ship's cook.

Then, when we got back to New York, 'Dickie' Bird arrived to take up the job of our Chief Engineer. He knew the ship, having sailed in her before, and he had a bit of a nasty reputation – in fact it took him about an hour to get on the wrong side of us. Even worse he upset our stokers as well and I am sure that at one stage, while we were at sea, one of them tried to do him some serious damage when a particularly heavy spanner fell through the floor grating to miss his head by an inch.

By the time we got back to New York we'd all had enough and to a man demanded to end our articles – refusing to sail with him on board. It caused a bit of a ruckus, with executives even being flown out from London to find out what was happening and why they had an officer's mutiny on their hands. We were all interviewed one by one and made our cases against Bird –

arguments which appeared to be accepted and he did apologise so we all agreed to sail again for one more trip.

When we got back to New York a new set of engineers was waiting to take over from us, and we were paid off and sent home. We travelled back on the SS United States, which held the Blue Riband for quick crossings of the Atlantic, happy though unaware that as far as Furness Withy as concerned, our cards were marked.

It was eighteen months before I could get another ship, and that was about the worst and most dangerous vessel – the SS Superiority – I ever sailed in. That lasted a month up in the Baltic before coming home and I paid off. It was the last ship I ever signed articles on, but I will always remember the Fort Avalon with so much affection.

It was a great time to be the age I was, in New York and on the North Atlantic. In fact, if I have to point to any particular year in my life it would be 1957/58, on that beaten up old tramp steamer that gave me so much in terms of pleasure and experience. Not simply because it was a 'hard drinking – hard playing' ship but, while over many years I have experienced great comradeship – I have never, before or since, felt camaraderie as deep and sincere as that we had on the Fort Avalon.

And talking of the Superiority...

YES – I PAID THE FERRYMAN

I had been warned. The guy in the Ship's Officers Pool emphasised that in no way would he offer one of their ships to any young Merchant Navy officer; but I was young, unattached and itching to get back to sea again, and on a coaster rather than go deep-sea again.

The fact that at the time there was quite a serious shipping slump on, is probably why I should have known better. The speed with which I was accepted – a telegram following an initial tentative enquiry – in the late 50s, should have had the warning bells going like the clappers. All I could see, though,

Still In My Own Lynchtime

was the telegram appointing me 4th Engineer on the SS Superiority and urging me to report to Greenhithe (on the Thames) with all speed.

I hurriedly gave a week's notice to King George's Hospital where I was maintenance engineer and packed my kit. Dad drove me across the Thames to the company's offices where, somehow, I had understood I would be joining my new ship. I was greeted with open arms and invited to stow my gear on board a ship that happened to be tied up on the jetty, but was very clearly not the Superiority.

Now I had emphasised in my letter that in no way did I want to join an oil tanker – which this near derelict wreck very clearly was (or at least had been in its day). I was assured that this was just a transit holding berth until the Superiority docked. Fair enough – I lugged my cases aboard and waited...and waited.

By 4 o'clock I was getting a bit worried. I had spent a lunch hour (or two) in a dockside pub with other in-transit chaps, but clearly the quicker I was aboard my new ship the better. Problem was there was very little sign of any more boats coming up the Thames. At 4.30pm I knocked at the shipping office door again and asked what was happening. Well, as one would, right?

Oh dear! Oh dear! They had forgotten completely about me. Yes the Superiority had docked... in Methil, near Kirkaldy on the Firth of Forth, and "Oh yes, here is your train ticket for the overnight train to Scotland."

Now this was a very disturbing little gem. Again I recalled the smirk on the face of that Officer's Pool bloke who'd warned me about this particular company. Still as I have said, I was young, unattached and totally bloody stupid, so off I dashed to London laden down with my gear.

There were only two of us in the compartment that night as we rattled towards the Land of the Rising Haggis, and as it happened he was also a merchant seaman. He was on his way home to Newcastle after signing off a ship in the Albert Dock, so we kept each other company happily chatting and drinking his duty free Scotch as we chugged north through the night. By the time he got off on Tyneside I was having a bit of a job keeping my eyes open but I had to change at Edinburgh, so I forced myself to stay awake.

It was a pretty grim, cold and misty, February morning when I got off the local train from Edinburgh onto Kirkaldy station. Both Kirkaldy and I were, to put it mildly, tired and dirty, so it didn't help matters much to find no taxi-service at the station. I was directed to go to the nearest bus stop where I could get a morning workers bus to Methil Docks.

Docks are easy to find. All you look for are masts and cranes, and keep an ear out for the seagulls, so actually finding them once I had been decamped from the bus outside the gates wasn't a problem. I staggered along the dockside, weighed down with cases, holdalls and my portable Dansette (record player), looking for my new ship. Suddenly I came to a part of the dockside that sort of stopped. It restarted some thirty or so yards further on, but that narrow gap had a few million gallons of the Firth of Forth flowing through it, and there seemed to be a marked lack of bridges in the neighbourhood.

A somewhat scruffy looking individual was standing nearby. Since he wore a thick roll neck jersey and peaked cap, I guessed he might be a good bet to ask if the Superiority was in port and, if so, where the hell was she.

He thought for a moment, and then pointed vaguely through the mist, across that watery void, and telling me in thick Anglo-Gaelic, that there was a ship on the other dock over there that might well be the one I was looking for. Great, but how do I reach it? He revealed I was lucky – he was 'the ferryman', and all I needed to do was get my gear into his boat and he would row me across the gap to the other side.

Easy, huh? Well, yes – but I am here to tell you that this was no Woolwich Free Ferry. First you had to climb down an iron-rung ladder that was fixed to the wall of the dock into his boat. Then you had to stand in it as he lowered your luggage down to you on the end of a rope. That done, he joined me in the boat, rowed the few yards across, stuck his hand out for a quid, and then tied my luggage back onto the rope for me to pull up once I had climbed another ladder. onto the dockside. Nothing to it really – especially for a guy who had been awake for the best part of 24-hours and had travelled the length of the land on a train and bottle of whisky.

Eventually I stood, luggage stacked around me, on the other dockside as my ferryman rowed back. I found myself staring with growing unease, turning to horror, at the shape that was emerging out of the thinning mist. It was indeed the 3,500-ton SS Superiority – its obviously once-smart yellow livery now liberally smeared with a thick coating of Polish coaldust. Even as I watched winches working on the hatches were hauling out tons of loose coal, some of it spilling out and dropping in great chunks onto the deck More of that acrid black dust filled the air, and more of the ship, with a choking vapour as the cranes and winches filled the dockside coal-trucks. I looked back – the ferryman had vanished back to the other side of the dock.

Without a shadow of any doubt the steamship Superiority was the filthiest and scruffiest dog of a vessel I had ever seen, let alone signed articles on. It was a floating slum and I was its 4th Engineer. I must have been stark, staring, and bloody mad.

In fact, after a month of sailing round the Baltic, in mid-winter, on a ship with a freshwater tank on the upper deck, which needed unfreezing every morning, a cabin that became awash with sea-water whenever the slightest sea was running and a cook whose skill and concept of hygiene would have done credit to an Albanian squat, I was quite enthusiastic about signing off her again.

During that four weeks we'd had armed guards on the gangway to stop us seeing Poland, suffered a second-to-none chucking-out routine in a Danish pub, seas so exuberant I lost my denture to the North Sea through a bilge-pipe, and cooking so bizarre I lived on bread and onion sandwiches for the entire trip.

'Carry on up the Baltic' never even came into it. That quid I spent on the ferryman was the worst money I ever spent, that's for sure. I hadn't been seasick for almost three years – mainly because a maintenance engineer in King George's Hospital in Ilford, never really had to contend with storm-tossed seas and Baltic blizzards.

I have been in ships that had rolled, in some that had pitched and tossed, while a few had even done submarine impersonations in the slightest swell. I had never, until I joined the SS Superiority, been in one capable of every waterborne acrobatic known to man. Whoever had designed that bloody ship must have passed his Naval Architect exams by correspondence course, while living in the funny farm.

OK, so the geyser might never have appreciated that his little floating masterpiece would become a Baltic trader, when he positioned the freshwater tank on the upper-deck... with unlagged pipes. He might never have known that, within hours of leaving Scotland (in February) heading North, every toilet in that floating dustbin, apart from the engineer's one which was positioned above the main boiler, would be frozen solid -and we are talking salt water. frozen solid here not freshwater.

Even before we sailed, I had realised I was in a spot of bother, because I had met the ship's cook and had decided that a fairly strict 'bread and Spanish Onion' diet for the next three weeks might not be a bad idea. They were the only things I knew he would have kept his hands off because they came aboard before we sailed and neither needed his hands on them.

I had upset things from the start. As soon as I had staggered aboard and been introduced to the Chief Engineer, we had fallen out because I insisted in getting some sleep before I went near a boiler suit. That did not go down too well, but he had grudgingly accepted it after a bit of a barney. Then, just before we sailed, I had been ordered, as the ship's fourth engineer, to the galley to fix a leaking diesel pipe on the stove so the ship's cook could get on with dinner.

There he sat – Albert Steptoe revisited. Sitting on a stool in the middle of the galley, he was peeling spuds and tossing them over his shoulder into a large saucepan, clearly meant for dinner. Unshaven, he was dressed in a stained tartan shirt and dark shiny trousers and he wore a 'flat cap' that had clearly seen many a voyage; but the worst thing was that his aim was not too clever. More often than not the peeled spud would leave his, somewhat grimy, hand and completely miss its target. They kept falling into a puddle of diesel oil caused by the very leak I had been sent to stem.

Not to worry – the guy just picked the spud out of the puddle, rubbed it on the side of his shirt and threw it into the saucepan anyway. Eat your heart out Delia Smith, Ainsley Harrison et al. Well, it turns you right off your dinner, and anything else he is likely to cook, that sort of thing, right?

I decided that I would exist on sandwiches, which I would make – and in the event they turned out to be, in the main, onion sandwiches.

Anyway, we left Methil, and the Firth of Forth, enroute for Aalborg in Denmark. From there we were to sail to Stettin in Poland, still very much behind the Iron Curtain of course. Then it was back to Aalborg before returning to Scotland – to Glasgow on the Clyde – a three or four week voyage, in the middle of winter through some of the coldest and wildest seas in the business and in a tub that had disaster written all over her. (A year later her sister ship went down in the Irish Sea with all hands during a storm.)

I have already drawn attention to the fact that while I enjoyed the sea, my stomach did not. It wasn't long after leaving Scotland that I was back in the old routine of going down into the engine room armed with a bucket. Almost immediately I came to grief because, while I was cleaning out an oil filter, I vomited my front teeth denture, which disappeared out of reach into a bilge pump – and thence, presumably, into the North Sea. We bounced all the way to the Baltic.

For me Denmark was forgettable from the start. As we arrived I was still below shutting down the engine room as the dockies came aboard, and I had forgotten the elementary rules about locking cabin doors while in port. So I was burgled within ten minutes of being on Danish soil, losing my wallet and, even worse, a full bottle of Scotch I had brought aboard (non duty free) and, which I had not exactly been interested in during the turbulent voyage across the North Sea.

Then, just to make matters worse, I opened my wardrobe to check whether those thieving Danes had left me anything to find my luggage still there – floating in about a foot of seawater. Wonderful – of all the cabins in that ship, I got the one that with a leaking wardrobe.

I'll come back to Denmark, but Poland – well now that was a real education. By the time we got there, having clunked our way through hundreds of miles of Baltic ice-fields of 'frozen waves', I had a regular morning chore – unfreezing the water tank pipes.

Every morning, before breakfast and in whatever seas happened to be running at the time, I had to clamber up onto the upper deck in the freezing cold, wrap some paraffin-soaked rags around the pipes and set light to them. By the time we got to Stettin I was relieved that we were at least not heaving about all over the show. Yes, ok, we had a deep layer of snow all around us, but my innards could handle that.

That first morning I was up there wrapping my rags, and getting ready with the lighter, when I heard the unmistakable and still very familiar sound – marching boots. I knew that noise only too well – it wasn't that long since I had been a 'marching boot' myself doing the biz on barracks parade grounds. This lot though, seemed a lot more purposeful as I glanced up from my decktop 'bonfire'. It was a bunch of Polish squaddies, marching along the dockside towards us, and they were armed to the teeth.

They halted, an officer bawled out something totally incomprehensible, and one of his lads stepped smartly forward, rifle at the ready, to take his place at the foot of our gangway. He was our guard, clearly there to protect us, and to make sure none of us slipped ashore to go spying for the CIA. To be honest none of us had any intention of doing any such thing, but I tell you he scared the life out of us.

That night a coach with darkened windows took the entire ships company ashore, to go to the dock canteen for the only entertainment available in that miserable place. Everyone, that is, except me. I drew the short straw in the engineer's alleyway, and had to remain on board as Officer on Watch to run the generator and make sure the duty seaman adjusted the ropes holding us to the jetty as the tide changed.

I felt a bit sorry for the guy on the gangway, so when I made myself some hot chocolate and a bread and onion sandwich (I had maintained my diet), I made and offered him some as well, using sign language of course. He had been on duty for hours, keeping himself warm by occasionally marching up and down and stamping his feet, and it was a touch chilly out there.

As I offered him the sandwich and mug he glanced furtively around to make sure we weren't being watched. Then he grabbed the sandwich and shoved it into the pocket of his greatcoat before holding out his hand for the steaming cup I was proffering. Taking it, another swift glance around, and he swallowed the lot in one big gulp.

I kid you not – that stuff was so hot I was still sipping mine, but he threw his mugfull down like he had an asbestos throat, clearly keen to do so before his guard commander came back and spotted him fraternising with me. He grinned his thanks as he handed me back the mug, and I watched as he went back on sentry duty – surreptitiously shoving his hand into his pocket and coming out with pieces of the onion sandwich, which he shoved into his mouth like it was his last supper.

When we got back to Aalborg, after leaving Stettin, I got to go ashore – with the third engineer. All we had to do was remember that the Superiority was berthed in the 'Cement Fabrik' (cement factory), when it was time to come back aboard. Now you would think that was a simple thing, wouldn't you? Don't you believe it! It was Sunday and Aalborg was shut.

Drink we could buy – but proper grub other than the odd sandwich was definitely not on the cards. For me it was the defining moment – the last straw. Well almost.

We found ourselves a little bar in the middle of town and began some serious lager drinking. No food, just the drink and it went on for some hours but we had no real idea of just how late it was until the barman started stacking chairs. He was clearly sending a message, but it never stopped him serving us another two bottles of lager apiece.

Having done so, however, he then highlighted his previous message by opening the bloody door and letting the cool Baltic breezes blow in. OK, we picked up our bottles and wandered outside where, having carefully hidden our open bottles in our coat pockets he never saw the, we found a taxi.

'Cement Fabrik', we said – only to be met by a torrent of Danish. We had clearly met the only non-English-speaking Dane in town. He drove us to a police station where someone came out to interpret. The snow was snowing like a good un, and we were getting steadily more careless with the open bottles in our pockets. It turned out there were seven 'cement fabriks' in Aalborg – all we had to find out was which one.

There was only one way – we had to do a very expensive conducted tour of the docks until finally, enveloped in darkness against the snow, we spotted the Superiority. My colleague jumped out of the cab – I jumped out...tripped and went headfirst into a six-foot snowdrift. The taxi-driver helped pull me out, and then discovered that our lager had been fizzing out of our pockets all over his back seat for the last part of the tour. He was not best pleased – and neither were we when we got aboard to find all the power off and had to get boiler suits back on again so we could solve the problem.

Within hours of sailing from Aalborg for the dubious delights of the North Sea in the Superiority I was standing in the skipper's cabin telling him I was going to pay off his ship in Glasgow, and could I please have my docking bottle.

As a ship's officer in a coaster I was entitled to a bottle of Scotch duty free, but what I didn't know was that it was down to his discretion. He turned me down flat.

He burst into a tirade of personal insults into which I, my parents' marital status, and England, all came in for equal venom.

"*Ye'll ne'er grace my ship again,*" he screamed in raw and furious Scots. That did it – hanging grimly onto a stanchion as the ship sashayed her way back to Scotland – I went eyeball to eyeball with him.

"*The only fing that will give this ship any kind of grace is a bloody torpedo*" I yelled back in tortured Cockney. I was told later that our shouting match was heard clear through the ship.

The man never spoke to me again. Two days later we tied up in Glasgow and I was up on my toes and off down the gangplank, luggage, discharge book and cash in hand, heading for Kings Cross as fast as I could get there.

Whatever happened to the SS Superiority I never found out –

but a year later her sister ship, whose name escapes me, went down in the Irish Sea with all hands.

I can recommend to Weight Watchers the onion sandwich diet though. It may not be very social in terms of breath etc, but it worked for me. I should never have paid that ferryman in the first place, but sadly for me my sea career was over.

7

Dagenham Posted

No Spud in the fire

The old cliché that, 'its in the paper, so it must be true', carries about as much credibility as a party political broadcast, and I guess the scales fell from my own eyes as far as that's concerned very early on in life. It happened when I was sitting in a very boring maths class in Rosslyn Road School in Barking, and our teacher happened to glance across at a classmate who was gazing idly of the window.

"Good view out there, is it? He sneered, hurling the inevitable piece of chalk in his general direction.

"Yes sir!" At first the answer appeared a touch impertinent, and we all switched our attention towards what we expected would be a young ear getting whacked.

"Really? Well let us all in on the secret. What should we all be looking at then?" was teacher's sarcastic response. He never expected the reply he got.

"Well, sir, actually the roof of the dining hall is on fire". Within seconds we'd abandoned our desks and dashed over to his side of the classroom, just as the fire alarm sounded outside.

Yes, the dining hall was really ablaze. The roof of the place we would soon have been wrestling with rock peas, powdered mashed potato and the gravy marinated gristle that passed for meat in our school dinners then, had black smoke pouring out of

Still In My Own Lynchtime

it. Our classmate had been quietly watching it for a few minutes, but hadn't felt obliged to let the rest of us in on it.

We were hustled out and marched swiftly along the corridor and out into the playground. The police cars and fire engines had bells in those days, not the sirens they have today, and the streets around Rosslyn Road were already ringing as Barking's finest raced towards the thick pall of black smoke curling up into the sky by now. We had other arrivals swiftly on the scene too.

Despite the pubs already being open, it was soon wall-to-wall local reporters outside. They were very keen to talk to anyone, but they were more interested in talking to, or about, our teachers than us kids. Well, at first they were.

The fire wrecked the place. It had taken a real hold and proved conclusively that the school dinners they dished up to us in those days could be ruined even more, than when they were slopped onto our plates. The dining hall was on the upper floor of a building, which had the dual-use biology and physics laboratory on the ground floor. All were also well and truly gutted, that day and we all got an unexpected afternoon off because they sent us home for the rest of the day. The following day we made the national newspapers, because to earn a few extra shillings the local reporters had clearly passed on their stories and pictures to Fleet Street.

The Daily Mirror ran the story and picture on the front, and continued it inside the paper, and as an ex-journalist now myself I have to admit it was a great story anyway. They, however, were particularly keen on the story of 'Spud' Murphy, our biology teacher and his 'heroics'.

A former Battle of Britain pilot (he claimed), dear old Spud wasn't a bad teacher, as it goes; though he did often prefer to talk about the latest radio comedy shows like the Goon Show, than the exotic lifestyle of the amoeba.

The Daily Mirror reported how he'd dashed into the flames to rescue some mice that were kept in the lab. He had been forced back from the flames before having to give up his rescue attempt leaving the poor mice to suffer their fate. Great story – but it was also a pack of lies.

As it happened, the following day when they resumed school,

we had biology in an unscorched classroom, and Spud was clearly not a happy bunny. He pulled the Mirror from his brief case and denied the whole thing.

"I promise you all that this is total claptrap. All I told a reporter was that I had had some live mice in the lab, but I certainly did not give him this rubbish", he said indignantly.

He was right – he hadn't. But I know someone who had!

8

STORY

Eat your heart out, Emma Bligh

"Yes Emma, that's fine – I'll expect you here for lunch tomorrow at 12noon."

Justin Ffoulkes-Harris smiled happily as he replaced the receiver back on its gold and onyx base. Hardly stirring himself further, his well manicured hand groped along the back of the chaise longue to feel for the large single malt he had left there before answering Emma's call. He sipped the spirit delicately, savouring its smoothness and raising the glass in mocking celebration at the thought of the result that would come.

Her eager response to his suggestion of a quiet and intimate lunch hadn't surprised him, because he knew from experience what to expect. It had been a while since he'd discovered the rich treasures that lay in the 'lonely hearts' columns of the quality papers. As a result life had been good, as the expensive furnishings, clothes, paintings and silver 'objets d'art' around him clearly showed.

Yes indeed, in the last few years the wealthy, middle-aged and man-hungry ladies who'd advertised their desperation had paid dearly – and in fairness, usually willingly – for their expectations to be fulfilled. Justin, once better known to the Metropolitan Police as 'Silverlips' Johnny Harris, had come a long way from his Dagenham childhood and juvenile detention-centre days.

Even his old fly-pitching to sell fake club ties and team photos outside Upton Park on match days, seemed an age away. West Ham might often still languish in the doldrums, but the born again Justin was definitely in the premiership class when it came to stylish living.

He stretched out along the chaise longue and raised his glass again in salute to the lady who was about to be added to his list of conquests. "Eat your heart out, Emma Bligh. You are in for a couple of glorious weeks, and I know you can afford it my love" he laughed.

That much he knew because at their first lunchtime meeting in the Hilton Hotel's restaurant in Park Lane, he'd established everything about her that he needed to know. The jewellery, the clearly expensive clothes that she did no justice to, the amount of perfume she had been wearing and even the source of her apparent wealth.

To his experienced eye this all said 'rich, no class and desperate'; but he knew how to play his catch and had made no move, other than to invite her to call him when she was next in town. That she had just done, and now he was sure she was swimming into his net.

Sure enough, just before noon the following day Emma was pressing the doorbell to his Limehouse riverside apartment. A small, 'dumpyish' brunette with lips thickly smeared in deep scarlet and clearly the wrong side of forty, she was wearing a plain blue dress. It was enough to emphasise her ample proportions, but with enough bosom exposed to confirm Justin's estimate of her determination to get a man.

She was also wearing perfume that, while it might not have been expensive had probably never been intended to be sloshed on by the bucketful. It was overpowering and filled the place with all the sensuous stench of cheap deodorant.

Brazenly ignoring the attack on his nostrils Justin gave her a very welcoming embrace, giving her a peck on her cheek before helping her off with her coat and handing her a glass of chilled Chardonnay.

They smiled as they greeted each other – but perhaps for different reasons. She was clearly impressed with the

Still In My Own Lynchtime

surroundings, while he was just as quick to spot hers. He quickly summarised the value of the rings, the pearls hanging from her neck, the diamond brooch sparkling from a bosom and the thick gold bracelet on one wrist, with the equally valuable Longines watch on the other.

These are the little things a man notices – well as least, a man like Justin Ffoulkes-Harris does. "Money, but no class", he muttered to himself as he smilingly escorted her to the balcony overlooking the river where a magnificent lunch, courtesy of the local deli, had been laid out ready. This was the bait.

There can surely be nothing so relaxing as lunch on a fine day overlooking the Thames. The smoked salmon and king prawn salad, the wine and the 'designer-chat' that Justine was so skilled at – all contributed to breaking down the barriers, and his guest very soon got really talkative.

Apparently Emma Bligh lived in a small and isolated cottage in Tiptree, an Essex village about eight miles from Colchester. She'd spent most of her life there, mostly looking after her parents until they'd been killed in a road accident almost a year earlier. Now she was alone, with a little money, and a small bookshop her father had left her.

"A bookshop?" he queried. Somehow, that seemed disappointing, but she smiled reassuringly.

"Well, it's not an ordinary bookshop. I deal in rare books – first editions, real collector's items", she told him. Justin could hardly believe his ears and as she went on to explain about the value of some of the books she dealt in. As she spoke he felt his prospects rising by the minute, especially since it began to be a two-way exchange of information, for she suddenly started asking questions herself.

"What about you, Justin? What do you do for a living – because whatever it is you are clearly very good at it", she waved her half-filled glass at the room. It was a question he was ready for – indeed, but for a few relevant points, it had been one he'd been leading up to. His response had been well rehearsed over the years.

"Emma, like you I was orphaned too, but in my case it was when I was very young. My parents were murdered in Southern

Rhodesia, by terrorists who wanted our farm. An aunt brought me to London, and raised me here. She actually became one of the early lottery big winners, and as a result we had a great lifestyle. When she died two years ago, she left me everything", he told her.

He was quite glib with the explanation which he felt covered every angle, and Emma was clearly very impressed and sympathetic especially about how he had lost his parents. In fact his parents were still alive, well and living in Basildon, but the similarity between Emma's genuine loss and his own fictitious one, was very deliberate once she'd told him about her parents. Now that she thought they really had something in common, she was putty in his hands. He even lied shamelessly about doing voluntary work in a local hospital.

The time passed quickly and soon, she was glancing at her watch indicating it was time for her to go. He pressed her to have another glass of wine, but she shook her head.

"No, Justine! I am still a working girl and I still have some people to see in the West End", she said, explaining that she had to meet an important buyer that afternoon before continuing.

"In a sense, I've been mixing business with pleasure this afternoon – a lot of pleasure, I might add", she smiled. He took her to the door to say goodbye, and was about to move to stage two of his plan and organise another meeting, when she stopped and turned to face him again.

"Justin. I really have had a lovely time today and would like to return your hospitality in some way. Are you busy on Sunday", she asked. He could have hugged her there and then but pretended to think about it for a moment before replying.

"Busy? No, actually I should have been working at the hospital this weekend, but I did some shifts for a friend last week and he is repaying the favour by doing mine" he told her.

"Good! Then come to lunch at the cottage, and I will cook", she said. A clouded look passed across his face. "What's wrong?" she asked.

"I'd love to Emma, but I've got a bit of a transport problem this weekend. My car is having a major overhaul in the garage, and I won't get it back until the middle of next week. I don't like trains, so perhaps we could leave it for a week", he said, sensing she would not hear of it anyway. Nevertheless, even he was taken by surprise at her next proposal.

An offer he couldn't refuse

Laying her hand on his arm, she looked up intensely into his face. "Look, my Volkswagen is downstairs in your car park, and I won't really need it until next Monday. I can use the underground to do my business this afternoon and then go home by train. So suppose I leave it here and you use it to come to Tiptree on Sunday. Oh Justin, please say you'll come", she pleaded. She was so obviously besotted now that he decided to play still a little harder to get.

"I'd love to – but how do I get home again after lunch on Sunday?" he queried. She smiled with those crimson-framed teeth again.

"Well, let's not worry about that – I can put you up at the cottage on Sunday night, and then run you back here on Monday when I am back in London to do some more business". She said it with a trace of coyness and promise in her voice, as she thrust her car keys at him.

He hesitated, but only for effect, before responding. "Emma, you are very kind, and I will accept your offer", he said as he took the keys.

He kissed here as she left, of course. He'd intended it to be a formal peck on the cheek again, but at the last moment she turned her face full on to his lips and returned the kiss with a passion that promised so much.

"See you Sunday," she breathed before turning out into the hall and vanishing down the corridor.

She was gone, yet the overbearing stench of that dreadful cheap perfume was still hanging in the air. He opened and closed the door rapidly a few times to try to dispel it but even so, as he went back into the apartment he could still smell it, cloying and heavily sweet, in every room. No matter – he had much to celebrate and a great weekend to look forward to. Even better he was confident that Miss Emma Bligh would soon be dipping into her bank balances on his behalf, and with that thought in mind, he could easily stand the sweet swell of her obvious success, pungent though it was.

For Justin next few days passed in a haze of anticipation. He even had a car to use, though sadly Emma hadn't filled the petrol tank before lending it to him so he'd had to pay for that. Soon it was Sunday morning and, armed with his usual 'ground bait' of flowers and chocolate.

Justin started to make his way out of London along the A13 and the M25. Then it was on to the A12 near Brentwood, and within the hour he was leaving that road to follow the signs to Kelvedon and on to Tiptree and Vine Cottage.

The place was exactly where she said it would be – just past the windmill on the left – and at the end of a small track. It was certainly secluded, and the thatched roof, lattice windows and well-kept garden also spoke for themselves. As he pulled up outside, for the first time, even the faint thoughts of potential marriage began this time began to cross his mind.

He'd half expected her to come rushing to the door to greet him, but she didn't. As he approached it he saw it had a small pale blue envelope with his name on it pinned to it. Tearing it open he read the letter inside.

"Justin!" it began. "Please forgive my not being here to greet you, but I have had to pop out for an hour or so. Early this morning I had a phone call from an important client in Colchester. He is leaving for America later today and is in urgent need of a book he ordered from me. Since this book is worth several thousand pounds I cannot afford to ignore the business, so I called a cab and popped over to his hotel". The words 'several', 'thousand' and 'pounds' had seared themselves into Justin's brain as he read them. He turned to the second page of Emma's note.

"I will try to be back for lunch, but if not I will certainly be here by mid-afternoon. If you came in from Kelvedon, you will have noticed a little pub just before the crossroads called the Kings Arms, where you can get a good lunch. I have its number and I

Still In My Own Lynchtime

will call you there if it looks like I am going to be delayed further. Sorry dear, but I will make it up to you later. Love, Emma B".

Justin smiled to himself – he had no problem with any of that, because it meant his hostess would feel under an even bigger obligation when she did arrive. He tucked the note into his jacket and, since it was a nice morning, decided to stretch his legs and walk back to the pub rather than drive.

She was right about the pub too – it was a nice little place and the landlord turned out to be a very friendly chap. He cheerfully sold Justin the pint and a pie he'd ordered before settling down to enjoy the Sunday paper he had brought from London.

About half an hour later the landlord called over to him. "Excuse me, sir. Are you Justin?" He nodded that he was, to be told there was a phone call for him in the next bar. He walked through and picked up the receiver – it was Emma, and she was very apologetic.

"Oh, Justin, I am terribly sorry about this, but I'm having a few problems with this sale that I never expected, but I hope to be with you by half past two at the latest", she told him.

He reassured her that he was fine, and that he understood the unexpected twists and turns of the business world. "Don't worry love, I will be here when you arrive".

Emma thanked him for being so considerate. "I should have left you the key, but I really didn't think I would be long" she said. He told himself that that would have been nice, because it would have given him more opportunity to explore his options while she was out, but kept the thought to himself.

"Relax Em, it's a fine day, and you were right. They do serve a good pint here," he laughed as he put the phone down, ordered another pint and went back to the other bar to carry on reading his newspaper.

Over the next couple of hours he ordered several more drinks and started to forget the time – in fact by three o'clock he was feeling a touch drunk. He realised that Emma was probably back home now, but had waited to keep her on tenterhooks a little longer before walking, or rather staggering, back to Vine Cottage. When he got back though she still wasn't in, so he sat in the car for a while. It wasn't long before a combination of the beer and the warm sunshine, he nodded off.

It was almost dark by the time he woke, and for a confused second or two, he wondered where he was. There was no light on in the cottage, and from what he could see through the windows as he peered through them nothing was moving inside either. Surely she wasn't still tied up with her customer in Colchester. Now he began to get a bit angry – but it was an anger still tempered by the thought of how guilty she would feel when she did arrive. This, he felt, was another thing he could turn to his advantage. Why not go home to London and let her get into a real guilt trip, thinking he had given up on her? Anyway, if the worst came to the worst, he still had her car.

He was already visualising the moment when his 'indignation' would turn to forgiveness. It almost guaranteed a flood of nice presents to make up for her churlishness. Oh, yes, things could turn out very nicely after all.

Homeward bound, he was hardly back onto the A12 before a nasty experience in the shape of an Essex Constabulary car appeared in his rear mirror, clearly requesting him to pull over. Without really thinking about it, he did so, and was stunned when the copper asked him to breath into the breathalyser.

He'd forgotten the drink, and now that afternoon's intake of ale showed itself, and he was clearly way above the limit. He was arrested and taken to Witham Police station where he was blood tested and charged. It meant him spending the night as a guest of the nick, until the alcohol cleared his bloodstream of course. Then, after being released, he had to call a cab to make his way back to the car, which was still in the layby on the A12.

He decided to go back to Vine Cottage, where he fully expected Emma to have spent an anxious night unable to make contact with him. To his surprise the cottage was as empty of life as it had been the day before. He decided to go back to London.

Despite everything, he was still happy when he got home. He was still relishing the Emma Bligh guilt trip he was relying on to be a bountiful one as far as he was concerned. In his imagination he could almost hear the telephone ringing inside as he reached the front door of his apartment. He walked in and without really thinking, headed for his gold and onyx telephone – then he stopped dead in his tracks. It was gone.

In fact everything was gone – furniture and furnishings, pictures, ornaments and objets d'art – the lot. While he was out he'd not only been burgled, he'd been cleaned out. The whole place had been stripped bare, with even the fridge and cooker unplugged and removed. Only two things remained.

An Avis rental form for a Volkswagen, made out in his name, lay on the floor, and a sickly smell of cheap scent hung heavily in the air.

9

VIEWPOINT

Yes, laugh at them – because they're fools

'It was upsetting to hear what she had taken before – Leah had experimented with speed and tried cannabis. I sat there thinking we must not let this tarnish Leah. I was still proud of her. She was an ordinary kid who had tried what lots of other kids had done. She was not a drug addict...' (Janet Betts)

In November 1996 two Essex people took one of the most courageous decisions any parent has had to face. They deliberately encouraged the media to use the last photo of their dying daughter as a public shock therapy designed to show as wide an audience as possible the terrible consequences of her last Ecstasy tablet. The awful expressionless face of Leah Betts filled TV screens and newspaper pages just as Paul and Janet Betts hoped it would when they put their own personal grief to one side in an attempt to save 'ordinary' kids.

Since that time Paul and Janet Betts have never stopped campaigning to bring home the message they themselves learned so tragically and unexpectedly. Now based in Scotland for years they still tour schools, give talks to a variety of groups and appear in front of cameras and microphones whenever they get the chance. I am very proud to have known them, and in a journalistic way supported them.

Yet all those years on, kids are taking pills, sniffing powders or injecting chemicals into their bodies. We rail against it, and the merchants of death who make fortunes from this miserable and deadly trade. We even silently applaud the murder of those who are clearly involved in this industry, but who have fallen out or breached someone else's 'turf'.

Yet the media talks glibly of 'recreation drugs' as though some are harmless – and the excusers (many themselves users) draw comparisons between 'legal' drugs like alcohol and tobacco, as though that provides a justification of some sort. Booze dealers, as a general rule, do not shoot each other and nor do they target children.

There can be no justification. The fact that we smoke cigarettes (I don't) and drink whisky (I do) should not be used as a way of making other forms of drug abuse – even cannabis – appear acceptable and excusable. But what do we do?

We increase police activity on the street and fill the jails with stiffer and longer sentencing. As long as there is a consistently new growth market however, the dealers will crawl out of the woodwork to take advantage – even outside schools, let alone the youth clubs.

We must tackle this problem at source – and I mean really at source, by going back to the hearts and minds of the kids who provide the dealers with their market. If we spent a fraction of the money we pour into investigation, arrest, prosecution and incarceration reaching out to, not preaching at, the kids – that would be a real investment. It would pay immense dividends in all areas of our society and perhaps save their lives.

There is no point in writing, designing and producing a million leaflets warning children of the dangers of drug taking – most of them know the dangers. Sadly, like many of us, they believe it is the kind of thing that happens to others rather to them, themselves. They tell themselves they can handle it!

There is only one real fear that has any kind of effect on young minds – peer pressure and the fear of being thought inferior, physically or mentally. That is where we should be concentrating as a nation.

Those of us who grew up before the sixties remember how we

were mind-conditioned (brainwashed if you like) with 'wholesome' comics like the Wizard, Hotspur and Champion etc. Their heroes were role models who only ever fought fair. Rockfist Rogan never kicked a man in a fight and he would have scorned anyone who did – neither would he have swallowed, sniffed, puffed or injected a chemical of any format.

Things have changed of course, and today's pre-teens and teenagers are more sophisticated than we ever were. They are also more exposed to more real life on TV etc than we ever would have seen. Yet there is one area that worked for us, and would still work with today's young people, though it might seem a little harsh in our featherbedded society. We would have to recognise that Leah, and the other victims since, were 'Wallies'.

It is a word that Peckham's Del Trotter would recognise, along with its compatriot 'plonker' Even the Oxford English Dictionary sees it as a word to describe a 'foolish or inept person'. How else can you describe a person who takes a chemical into his/her body, knowing that it carries the risk of self-destruction?

Children, even from a very early age, do not ever want to be seen as figures of fun by their contemporaries. Spike Milligan's Goon character 'Eccles' was a great joke, but few of us would welcome being seen or described as an 'Eccles'. Children, (and some of us can even remember that far back), do not even like being seen as 'dunces' or 'weaklings', let alone as a 'Wally'.

So we must condition children's minds to the point where they see that anyone taking a drug, not prescribed by a doctor, is a Wally to be laughed at. Mockery – as governments in the sixties, when they were at the mercy of satirists like Peter Cook, David Frost and Monty Python, discovered is a powerful weapon. It is one we should not reject out of sympathy for the addicts already hooked.

I am not suggesting such pathetic figures should be abandoned or denied treatment if they genuinely want it; far from it. It is time though to forget the lost causes, and spend some of the resources we waste on them on preventing more lost causes developing in the playgrounds of the future. Brainwash, mind condition, promote – call it what you like, but show the addicts up for what they are and to hell with their feelings.

If you get the kids laughing at the 'wallies who take drugs' – they will not want to become one, and be seen as one, themselves. Lets laugh at them, because they're fools.

10

Dagenham Posted

The Globe, theatre of dreams

You can't go through life without meeting someone about whom you can truthfully say it was 'hate at first sight'. Someone who you feel has scarred you for life in some way or another, and yeah, I've had a few of them!

I guess Hitler was the first. From an early age we were mocking him by sticking a finger under our nose, holding an arm up in mock salute and goose-stepping all over the playground. We were doing that long before Basil Fawlty, and if the Wehrmacht had turned up in 1940 they would probably have got the hump over that little habit.

In school there were one or two, like the 'fearsome Frau' – the German born Mrs Morrison. She did her best to blitz some knowledge of her native language onto our tongues (when she wasn't battering us against the wall blackboard with her clumping right hook). There was also a teacher called Campbell who tried to get me the cane because I jumped onto a 106 bus before he could, and claimed he had been in front of me at the bus stop.

But it wasn't until I'd actually left school and started an engineering apprenticeship (at a wage of 35 shillings – £1.75 a week) at the Globe Pneumatic Engineering Company in Chadwell Heath that I met a man who to this day I hate with a passion that even the odd touch of arthritis cannot curb. Yet, it is probably unfair because the guy was only doing his job and since, as an engineering apprentice, I was about as useful as a knitted hammer, I probably just resented his doing it on me.

His name was George White and he was the senior foreman in the factory, so no one liked him anyway. My first supervisor however was a guy called Fred Gilham, who was the 'charge hand' for the fitting and assembly shop where they put pneumatic hoists and drills together. Fred, in fact, was the man I perhaps should really have hated, bearing in mind the job he opened my working career with. He did seem to be a fairly friendly and reasonable sort of chap though.

That first hour or so he showed me around the factory, which made pneumatic hoists, drills and other compressed air-driven machinery. There were two long and noisy workshops filled with benches, drills, lathes, grinding and milling machines – all of which meant nothing to me at the time, except that they all contributed to the general clatter.

After explaining that we would have ten-minute tea breaks mid morning and mid afternoon, with an hour for lunch, he took me towards a small waist-high galvanised metal tank. It was half full of what proved to be paraffin, and beside it was a flat barrow piled high with cardboard boxes. They turned out to contain some metal bearings that, even to my inexperienced eye, were clearly of some considerable age.

They consisted of a split outer ring, about two inches deep, while inside was a complex set of wheels on rollers. The company had bought these cheaply from the War Office because they were fifty years out of date (this was 1950 don't forget). At some stage they'd had a coating of preservative wax on them and apparently it was my job to clean all that off in the paraffin bath and put a coating of modern grease on them. The ones that proved to be really rusty underneath the preservative I had to dump, but the better ones had to be greased and re-packed for use in the pneumatic hoists the Globe was making.

As long as I live I will never forget those bearings and that bloody bath of paraffin. Day after day I scrubbed away with a wire brush, and whenever I thought I'd finished one lot, Gilham appeared on the horizon with another barrow load from the stores (where he had a thing going with the stores lady). After a few weeks scrubbing, a layer of oily black slime began to build up in the bottom of the tank, and with every new batch I was lumbered with, that layer got deeper, thicker and slimier.

Half way through the morning a whistle would blow, and we would all sit down near our machines and benches for a mug of tea. I would eat my sandwiches after rubbing some of the slimy paraffin off my hands with an oily rag.

Around me, as I was scrubbing away in paraffin like a demented wick, hoping no one would throw a lighted match in my direction, other apprentices (the Globe had realised what nice cheap labour we made) were being taught the art of painting engine cases, or watching metal bars being sawn, and lathe tools sharpened. They never knew the joys of 'finger skinny dipping' in sludge and the painful scraping of fingers with a wire brush.

Lunch breaks in summer meant we could sit outside and eat our sandwiches with our oil stained fingers. During the winter we would sit around those great glowing iron stoves that were used to heat the factory and toast them sandwiches on the end of handmade toasting forks.

One day I noticed that the skin on my hands was starting to peel off, and itch like crazy. Now, finally, I had a reason to complain to Gilham. Nowadays of course someone in the position I was would go and talk to their solicitor first, but this was the 1950s, not the 21st century.

I had spent four months in that paraffin bath scrubbing away at his bearings, and now I could agitate for change on medical grounds. I even joined the Amalgamated Engineering Union, but they weren't over anxious to call the factory out on strike over my peeling digits. To be fair, Gilham was very concerned and insisted on a change.

'Tip that stuff out, scrub the tank clean and get some clean paraffin before you do any more bearings', he ordered.

Still, there was one minor compensation – I had served my first three months as an apprentice, so they signed my articles and my wages went up to two quid a week. Eventually I even got to paint the engine cases.

To this day I will never fully understand how I allowed Dad to talk me into going into engineering, which I hated. At school my metalwork had been on a par with my woodwork – dire – and the idea of working in a smelly and noisy factory had never really appealed anyway. I had wanted to be a newspaper reporter, not a boiler-suited roller bearing scrubber. The Globe was my theatre of dreams – day dreaming of the day I would be out of it.

Admittedly I did eventually get out of the paraffin bath and onto some machinery – capstan and centre lathes, but they were in George White's own domain and he was always the down side.

As it turned out there were some positives that resulted. Without that experience I would not have had the self-claimed skills to get into the Merchant Navy and that would have meant losing some of the best years of my life. About three years after I started at the Globe I went into the Royal Navy to do my national service, and when I was demobbed I did go back to the Globe, and George White, for about six weeks. That was enough.

I had the necessary qualifications to bluff my way – George and the Globe had given me the incentive – into signing articles on the MV Southern Prince, as a Junior Engineer Officer. Thanks George!

11

Some long and winding roads

Walking home with Dearly Beloved and our first two nippers, Tracey and Debbie, shortly after we came to Brentwood in the late sixties we came across the Blue Line taxi service in Hart Street (now part of the Ropers Yard shopping area). Purely on impulse I ambled in and asked if they had any part time vacancies I could fit in with my London day job in the Birmingham Post and Mail's Fleet Street office.

Colin Page, the guvnor, asked if I knew Brentwood and lying shamelessly I assured him I knew it like the back of my hand. On the way home I bought a street map of the area, and spent the rest of the day trying to learn it.

Early next day, albeit somewhat nervously, I turned up to be shown how to start a diesel taxi, operate the radio and how to charge by the mile because these cars had no meters. Then he told me to go down the station taxi rank because George, his regular driver there, was in hospital.

Warily I drove into the High Street and almost immediately, before I'd even reached Kings Road to turn left, a guy put his hand out, jumped in and told me he wanted to go to the station. This was a real result with half a crown for me, since I was on my way there anyway, and by the time I dropped him off, I was already getting confident.

A queue of taxis was waiting for the morning rush hour trains, and whenever one turned up a crowd of commuters emerged to make a dash for us, asking to go to places like Fords (Warley),

Shenfield or the High Street. My first one threw open the rear door, plonked himself down onto the backseat and said: 'Harlow, please!'

Harlow? I never even knew what rough direction it was, and it certainly wasn't on my street map. But before I could come up with some kind of lame excuse, a 339 bus pulled away from the bus stop on the other side of the road with 'Harlow' emblazoned on its destination board. Whew!

I did a U-turn to fall in behind my public transport trailblazer, and tracked it up Kings Road and into the High Street, being careful not to overtake it of course. Fortunately Brentwood at that time of the morning was full of traffic so it didn't look unusual to a newcomer. He would not have known about the short cut through Western Road into Ongar Road, cutting the High Street out completely, any more than I did.

I quickly realised that I would soon be out of radio contact with base as well, so made a quick call to find out how much I should be charging for the journey; but no one in the office was quite sure. They hazarded a guess at 'two or three quid', before they faded into the ether leaving me still following that bus along Ongar Road, through Pilgrims Hatch, Kelvedon Hatch and all the way up to Ongar itself.

By then my passenger had twigged that the bus in front was going to the same town he wanted, but slower. He began to ask awkward questions about my obvious reluctance to overtake it, so I reassured him that this was a noted dangerous road and no one took any chances on it.

We crawled out through Ongar – thankfully just as crowded as Brentwood High Street had been – and turned left at the Four Wantz roundabout where I started to get cocky, because I was seeing Harlow road signs. Unfortunately, the bus had picked up speed too, and I couldn't get past him in my slow to respond diesel cab. Now, when you reach the crossroads (now roundabout) where you turn left for North Weald and Epping, you carry straight on to reach Harlow. How was I supposed to know that? I was still following that bloody bus.

We rattled through North Weald and even into Epping, which was where I had to admit I was a newcomer to Harlow and

Epping. Well, how was I supposed to know the bus route went into Epping, and then out again for the last mile or so to Harlow. My passenger was now almost an hour late for work by the time we reached Harlow.

My fare never knew where he wanted to go, so we had to ask a local copper to show us where it was before I could drop him, but the guy never left me a tip. It was a good job I made that first half a crown and overcharged him anyway.

During our child-rearing years especially I did a lot of extra part time work to supplement my wages and to help buy the mountains of baby food, piles of nappies and then bagfuls of uniforms. Without question the taxi-driving was one of my favourite jobs though and in fairness it did teach me a lot about the geography of Brentwood (and its distance from Harlow) as well as helped me meet a lot of people.

At this stage I suppose I ought to casually drop the information that I once had Fred MacMurray, the Hollywood actor, in the back of my cab. He was working in England and was visiting friends in Shenfield when he plopped into the back seat of my cab at the station. Good tipper actually, but not a great conversationalist.

I would usually work the mornings, because my Birmingham Post shift never started until 2pm usually, but all day on Saturday was very lucrative. In the early days especially I had the station rank job, but a lot of our time was spent in the office waiting for people to phone in with jobs, or just stagger in with their shopping bags begging to go to Hutton or Warley.

I was with Blue Line for a couple of years and I remember once being talked into working a Sunday evening (mainly a pub run of course). It was during the winter and I was just about to do my last run when a call came over the radio asking me to come back to base to pick up a fare.

I wasn't too happy about that – and even less so when the fare turned out to be an American airman, who wanted to get back to his base in Weathersfield which is up in the wilds of north Essex. (Now an RAF base). However I was assured that not only was it a good fare, worth about five quid which was a lot then, but I could take the cab home and bring it back the next day.

Well, anything to help the Yanks, so I went back to Hart Street and picked him up. He assured me he knew the way anyway and he seemed like a nice bloke, so off we went up the A12. I seem to recall we branched off somewhere near Colchester and while my passenger had seemed good company I was a bit concerned by the fact that it had started to snow a bit.

In fact by the time we reached Weathersfield it was snowing quite heavily and I was not unhappy when Yank paid me off (handsomely as it happens), and I began to try to find my way back to the A12. We'd lived in Tiptree before coming to Brentwood so I knew the road very well once I got onto it, but my problem was trying to follow road signs pointing to Colchester, at gone midnight, and in a blinding snowstorm with the stuff settling heavily.

It was a nightmare journey but somehow I managed to locate Colchester and from then on it was a fairly easy chug (diesel engines were not noted for their speed then) along the A12 to Brentwood. I got home at one-o-clock in the morning, totally knackered, and all for a fiver and a packet of American cigarettes.

After a while Blue Line went all hire car and private cabbing so there was no space for us part timers, so I went down to the railway station were a chap called Johnny Morgan ran a company called Station Taxis. He was always looking for part time drivers and his little hut and yard by the station was only across the road from where we were living in Cameron Close anyway.

John was a great character – golf mad but with a sense of fun and whose girl friend seemed to run the firm anyway. He had some good school contracts too but his biggest problem was that his vehicles were not best maintained. I had a carload of kids once when it boiled over on the Southend Road and had to use a garage telephone to get him to send some help.

There was one run I did on a regular basis for him for which I had to pick up kids at various points and take them to a special needs school in Goodmayes. Good bunch of kids generally but they used to bully one lad – the tallest and meekest – quite mercilessly. In fact I had to stop the car a couple of times to tell them to leave the lad, whose name was Tim alone.

A few years later, when I was no longer driving taxis anyway, there was a very nasty murder in Brentwood. A Fords typist was brutally stabbed to death on a footpath by Shenfield Common. Her murderer was, I believe, actually turned in by his own sister or at least by a member of his family, and I was stunned to find out that it was Tim, the lad who had been so badly bullied in my car.

Eventually Johnny Morgan went bust so I went down Victoria Crescent where an old lady called Mrs Hammond also ran a local taxi business. She in fact offered the best deal of them all because you had half the take.

I was sitting on the rank one morning in one of her cars when Dearly Beloved rushed up to me with David, still a baby, in her arms. She was in a state of panic because she had some tablets, I forget what for, and she believed David had swallowed some of them while her back was turned.

I spent that morning rushing her up to Harold Wood hospital where David has his tummy pumped out and was examined by doctors for any ill effects. Fortunately there were none, and we came home again. It was great that I had the use of a car that day, but not so great that I had to go to Mrs Hammond and confess I had taken hardly any money.

The next day I was coming back from Hutton along Queens Road when a driver coming in the opposite direction suddenly turned into the Ursuline Convent School without realising I was passing it. He hit me smack in the side and did some considerable damage.

He did admit liability and I understand his insurance company did pay out for the necessary repairs, but Mrs H never seemed to need me driving for her after that week.

12

Liz and I

We met!
I was only just home from the sea,
She smiled, and factory gloom was lit
She laughed – the sound a joyous melody
In that moment I knew she was 'it'
That bright-eyed Essex beauty
Liz and I

We courted!
Our first date was to see Elvis,
Years later, we'd visit his home
But then, it was just to cuddle and kiss
Hand in hand, to wander and roam
Dreaming dreams, wishing our wish
Liz and I

We wed!
In St Margaret's, Barking, on a blustery day,
We made our lifetime vows,
Captain Cook had once trodden that way
Now we stood there, to make ours
Each pledging never to stray
Liz and I

We lived!
In a beaten up old caravan, lined
Up on a slaughterhouse base
With gypsies and travellers, but never mind
Yes it was a dump – a frightful place
But it had real people, the neighbourly kind
Liz and I

We bred!
Tracey, our 'Alka Selzer' Romford baby came first
Then, in Tiptree, Debbie turned up
David was next, on us in Brentwood he burst
Family complete? No, one more for the cup
Emma – 'Oh God, three girls!' I cursed.
Liz and I

We laboured!
To give our kids their chance in life
Both of us worked many hours
Not just as parents, but as husband and wife
Through life's sunshine, squalls and its showers
Happiness, sadness, and sometimes strife.
Liz and I

Still In My Own Lynchtime

We made it!
Despite it all, we lived our dreams
We'd coped with every hard test,
Showed we were one of life's great teams
Our family raised, left the nest
Each knowing what 'family' means
Liz and I

And now!
We've got the T-shirts, done it all
We can look back with pride
We made our bed – set out our stall
And travelled far and wide
And my God, we had a ball
Liz and I

13

STORY

Two birds – One stone

Its fair to say that it is not every day that MoMo and I get our collars felt, and especially on our own manor and even worse in our favourite boozer.

In fact, the CID in Market Street 'nick' itself was investigated more times than they'd come even close to putting us away. Big Maurice Morris (MoMo), behind his back – and Nicker Lambert had a reputation among the scallywags for our lack of convictions. So it was a bit of a shaker when McIver sent a pair of plod down to the White Horse with a pressing invitation to pop in and see him.

It had been a bit of a funny old day from the start, with the whole manor buzzing about the imminent arrival in the neighbourhood of the Lachlae Collection. Indeed I doubt if there was a villain anywhere on the patch who wasn't beating his brain out to come up with some way of liberating it, or at least one particular part of it. To be honest, even me and MoMo had been licking our lips a bit.

Well, it was tempting. The collection of Roman jewellery had been uncovered by some archaeologists working out near Colchester on the site of the historic Lachlae Manorhouse which was being lined up for a new Tesco's superstore. They had half anticipated finding the remains of an old Roman villa there, but

Still In My Own Lynchtime

had not expected to get a real bonus, buried beneath centuries of Essex dirt.

The old Roman geezer who'd once owned the villa had clearly not been short of the old drachmae, or whatever it was passed for readies in those days. Among the pottery and mosaics they had found his safe – a complete urn with a false bottom. They hadn't known about the false bottom until one of the archaeologists had dropped it and the contents had fallen out.

Most of it was fairly small time gear and coins, though there were one or three really quality bits of gold, silver and the odd precious stone, which his old lady had probably worn on fight nights at the Colchester Coliseum. Apart from one item the whole lot had been valued at around £10k and that was more to do with its history. But there was one exception.

Among her bits and pieces Mrs Roman Geezer had somehow got her hands on a huge gold brooch, in the centre of which was one of the biggest rubies you ever saw. In its day this piece of tomfoolery must have been a real star, and for some reason I never fathomed they'd called it the Cyrus Stone – and it was bloody priceless.

Possibly trying to justify the ratepayer's money they'd spent on digging the site up in the first place, the council had hit on the idea of sending the whole collection out on exhibition to banks all around the country. It was well insured and there was top security of course, but you know what they say – where there's a will, there's a sticky finger.

NatWest in fact was sponsoring the tour, and the whole lot would be arriving in our local branch in a week or so. Not unnaturally, a lot of local minds were turning over the possibilities of making a withdrawal.

I suppose that realistically, apart from MoMo and myself, there was only one other team on the patch likely to be able to lift the Cyrus Stone. 'Lo and behold' ten minutes before the rozzers came looking for us, it had walked into the pub and made straight towards us, with a nasty smirk on its nasty fat face.

'Nicker, my old son, and Maurice as well. How's yer luck, pals? Mind if I sit down', Armlock Harry Foster beamed.

'You are going to anyway, Harry, so feel free' I growled.

He plonked himself down heavily in the chair opposite us – a couple of his apes stood behind him trying to do a glare job on us, while the rest of the pub pretended not to notice. Well, that's the effect Armlock Harry Foster has on people.

We'd all been at school together, but Harry had come a long way since local racketeer Jackie Roberts, who he'd been 'minding', had managed to get himself into a cement mixer and then some office foundations on Canary Wharf. Harry, who'd once been a wrestler (hence the nickname) had taken over the rackets and clubs and, to be honest (not a word one likes using in nice company), had shown he had brains as well as brawn. We'd had a few run-ins in the past but we also had mutual respect for each other, and tried not to cross each other's path.

'Ah, that's better – my plates were killing me. Fancy a drink, chaps?' He signalled to one of his boys to do the fetching – but not the paying, because clearly this would be the landlord's treat. Much as Frank disliked giving out free booze he'd known he would be doing exactly that the minute Armlock had walked into his pub, but I shook my head.

'No thanks, Harry', I said, waving my almost full glass, 'What are you after anyway?'

He smiled that Heinrich Himmler smile he was renowned for, and held out his hands in mock salutation. 'Now, come on Nicker. There's no need for an attitude here – especially when I have come here specially to save you and Maurice from a nasty accident.'

'Accident? What sort of accident?' Mo had blurted out the question before I could stop him because I'd had the feeling we would not like the answer.

Too late – Armlock picked up the rather sizeable glass of Scotch that had found it's way to our table and sipped it thoughtfully, without taking his eyes off us. Then he carefully put it down again before continuing in that deliberately measured quiet tone of his.

'Well, Maurice, I am thinking of the kind of accident you and Nicker might suffer have if you make a play for the Cyrus Stone' he murmured, his beady eyes now fixed steadily on me. Idly I wondered how far I could push him.

Still In My Own Lynchtime

'It's a free country, Harry', I said airily, and with more confidence than I felt. He gave me that cheerless snide grin again.

'Very true, very true, Nicker my son, and long may it remain so. Especially for you two,' he muttered. Then he really took me by surprise.

His huge hand plunged into his jacket pocket, to emerge with a couple of really tasty looking Rolex watches. He tossed them casually onto the table where they lay, staring back up at us from a small puddle of best bitter.

'Look chaps think of these as a kind of small compensation, which you can have with my compliments. But in return you stay away from the Cyrus Stone. Is that crystal?' he glared and his voice hardened into a threat.

So that was it – Harry wanted to send his own troops in after the jewel and wanted to make sure there was no competition in the shape of Mo and myself. I was still not prepared to back down just like that, though.

'Come off it, Harry! Everyone in this pub knows Charlie Griffin got these tickers from that big house he turned over in Hampstead last month,' I said, nodding towards the bar where the rounded eyes of the rat-faced little fink in question was peering out from the top of a Chelsea scarf. Armlock grinned again.

'Again that could be very true, Nicker – but so what? You can still get fare money out of them from our favourite jeweller. What's more, the boys will come down to the station to help with your luggage, when you and Maurice take your well-earned rest on a Spanish beach', he grinned.

We both knew which jeweller he meant because of an incident a while back concerning the Rigby Tiara, but mention of it made me even more determined to brazen it out.

'And if I say we still ain't interested in watches or El Spainio?

Armlock took another swig. 'Me and the boys will come down to help when you and MoMo take your break anyway'. There was no doubting the menace in his voice with its emphasis on the word 'break'. Yeah, he had a way with words, did Harry.

He stood up, leaving the watches on the table with the little beer puddles lapping against them.

'Think about it, Nicker' he smirked, as he moved away with his apes in tow towards the bar. Maurice looked at me dumbly and picked up the two watches, which as it happens were not bad looking schmutter anyway. I think we both knew what we would have to do, and mentally started checking our passports.

It had been at moment that the coppers had walked in and, after glancing briefly around the bar, spotted us. Pure instinct had made Maurice drop the watches swiftly into his pocket as they'd walked in. Everyone in the boozer had listened as they verballed the invitation for Mo and me to accompany them to the station. It was also pretty clear they were not talking about the railway station, that Armlock had been talking about a few moments before.

Helping the police with their…

I glared at Armlock as we were escorted out of the pub and wasn't too pleased to see the look of pure joy on his face – it was that of a man who had just fitted us up.

'What's McIver want us for?' I'd protested, as we were bundled into the back of the panda. I was keen to keep their attention because Maurice was already stuffing the watches down the back seat of the car, but they blanked me anyway and the car moved off towards Market Street. In a matter of minutes we were being ushered into an office, and that surprised me a little as well because I had expected us to be sat down in separate interview rooms. Ten minutes later McIver strolled in, also looking like the cat that had swallowed the cream.

'Hello lads! Been keeping well?'

I was in no mood for small talk. 'What's all this about Mr McIver – we ain't done nothing'. The git grinned even more broadly, obviously thoroughly enjoying his moment.

'I know that Nicker. Oh, come on chaps – I just need your help for a few moments, that's all.'

'We ain't done nothing, seen nothing and heard nothing. If

you want grasses why don't you pop down to the garden centre, they've got a big selection there, I hear' I growled. He almost bust his ribs laughing.

'Nicker – don't get excited, son. You haven't been pulled for anything. I just want you to do something for me as a personal favour. All I want you to do is open a safe for me.'

Now I am a great supporter of the Monarchy, but if Her Majesty herself had walked in at that moment, I don't think I would have been more surprised.

'Come again?' I queried. He grinned back.

'The thing is Nicker, my wedding anniversary is today and sitting inside my safe there, is the fairly expensive – at least by my poorly paid policeman standards – necklace, I bought for the wife' he said, as he nodded towards the corner. He must really have enjoyed the look on my face by now, so he decided to explain further.

"To be honest Nicker, this is a bit embarrassing. While I was in court this morning the safe company's rep came on a routine visit to change the combination, and then left without leaving us with the new one. Yes, we change the combination here every three months on security grounds, just in case' he added.

Suddenly I was feeling confident enough to have a pop and be a bit flippant.

'Not surprised Mr McIver – considering all the evidence that goes missing from this nick from time to time' I said. His face tightened a little, but he made no comment, so I continued. 'Anyway what do you want me to do about it – can't you just phone for the new combination?'

'No. We've tried, but the guy is still out on his rounds and has his mobile switched off. Thing is, I am anxious to get the necklace out before I go off shift this afternoon so I can give it to her tonight over a celebration dinner. So I thought of you', he grinned.

'Why me? I ain't no peterman, McIver – you know that' He held up a reassuring hand to stop me, because he knew me too well.

'Nicker, my old son. I know you are not the absolute best in the business, but we put Kipper Malone away last year so you are the best available. You and Kipper were big mates at one time, and I'm sure he taught you a lot. So don't give me any old pony, son – just open the safe and you can go on your way. Don't forget, I'll owe you one'.

I was beat because the git knew he was right, but my whole reputation has been built on maximising opportunities, so I decided to haggle a bit.

'Well, just supposing I got lucky and did manage to get it open for you. What's in it for us?' I asked.

McIver sat and stared thoughtfully at me for a moment before sliding his hand into his pocket. It came out holding two very familiar, and tasty looking, Rolex watches.

'Funny thing is, Nicker, that after the lads brought you and Maurice in they started to clean out the car. Well it was a bit grubby, and guess what they found down the back of the seat. You know, I am sure I have seen items like this on a missing property list somewhere'. He raised his eyebrows questioningly, while in our case the sweat glands were going like the clappers now.

'Er look – we had nothing to do with them. We found those watches an hour ago in the pub, and we were about to bring them in to the nick as lost property', I muttered lamely. He gave me that reassuring smile again.

'I know that, Nicker. We know who to lift for that job anyway, but lets face it son, your dabs will be all over them and, er yes we had them dusted.' He knew I was whacked, so decided to throw me a morsel.

'Did you know chaps, that there is a nice little fifty quid reward on offer from the insurance company for these watches. If you help me, then I would have no problem with booking them in as being handed in by you, and putting you two up for the reward. Of course, the alternative – well, how does receiving stolen goods sound to you, Nicker?'

To be honest it wasn't much of a safe anyway and using the techniques dear old Kipper had taught me all those years ago it practically fell open. God, if only Kipper had stuck with me instead of getting carried away with the notion that he was a top

Still In My Own Lynchtime

class planner as well as a great cracksman, we could have made a fortune together. Still, that's another story.

McIver stood close, watching me as I tinkered with the combination dials trying to make it look as difficult as possible, and giving MoMo the chance to nick what appeared to be a couple of genuine warrant cards from the git's desk while I was doing so.

In no time at all the door of the safe was swinging open and McIver moved swiftly in, shoving me out of the way in his haste to get the velvet box I had spotted inside. Then he turned to me and opened it, showing it contained a really exquisite piece of sparkle.

'Thanks Nicker. Tell me, as something of an expert in these things, what do you think of this?' he asked.

For the first time since I'd been unfortunate enough to know him, I wondered if McIver was actually on the take. I was pretty sure that even his pay would not have easily funded the little bauble he was waving in front of me and which was clearly worth a fortune.

'Very nice, Mr McIver, very nice! Er, you mentioned a bit of bunce in reward money?'

'Ah yes, the money. Tell you what – I'll pay you myself right now, and get it back from the official reward dosh later. Fives ok?' I nodded dumbly as his hand dived into his wallet and emerged clutching fistful of beer vouchers. Disbelievingly we watched as he counted ten of them onto the table. The little pile lay there looking very inviting but just as I stretched out my arm to pick it up, he grabbed it to stop me.

'Nicker – look, it would not look too clever for us if this little episode got around the manor and I hope you realise that. In fact I think you ought to put it towards your holiday money – the little trip you and Maurice ought to go on first thing tomorrow morning'. Suddenly everyone was wanting MoMo and me to go on holiday.

'Your secret is safe with us Mr McIver, and I do hope the missus likes the necklace' I grunted, trying to pull my arm out of his grip. He held on to it and continued grinning.

'To be honest Nicker, what with the Cyrus Stone arriving on

- 95 -

the patch very soon, a brief holiday is probably not a bad idea, is it? I would feel a lot happier if the old firm of Lambert and Morris Ltd were off sea-fishing somewhere in distant climes' he said. Now I was livid because the coincidence of both him and Armlock making the same suggestion was too much. I was now totally convinced that McIver was bent.

'Oh yeah, how long you been on Armlock's payroll then? I thought that necklace was a bit pricey for a copper's wages' I sneered. His reaction was so violent I thought he was going to have a fit.

'Get out, get out!' he screamed in our faces. 'I don't need to get tangled up with the likes of you and Foster. On your bikes – and don't let me hear you are even thinking about coming back from the seaside until next month'. He was still shouting at us as we hurried down the corridor and out into the street.

On our way back to the White Horse, McIver's dosh was burning a pretty big hole in my pocket of course – but I couldn't get over the fact that both Armlock and McIver had told me and Mo to disappear for a few weeks. Fat chance! What they had done was virtually challenge us to lift that Cyrus Stone. 'We ain't going to let them down, Maurice me old mate!' I muttered, a number of ideas about how to do it already forming in my mind.

Armlock was still holding court in the pub when we walked back in. He waved cheerfully as I went to the bar for a couple of pints while Maurice found a table. 'What did they want, Nicker?'

'None of your business' I snarled, laying down one of McIver's fivers for the beer. I was just about to add a few more succinct and well-chosen words when McIver walked in – with some of his bogies. He was also a lot calmer than he'd been when we'd left him less than half an hour earlier.

Ignoring us, he walked straight over to Armlock. You could have heard a pin drop as he laid a couple of watches and a now very familiar velvet box containing a very nice diamond necklace, onto the bar He grinned and glanced at Charlie Griffin who was still with Armlock.

'Recognise these, Charlie?'

Griffin gurgled and choked but managed to shake his head. McIver ignored the protestation. 'I think you do Charlie, and I think perhaps we ought to discuss it down at the nick, don't you? he said. Then he really laid one on us listeners. 'Oh, you as well Foster'.

At that moment Armlock's fleshy face was a joy to behold. He was totally stunned.

'I had nothing to do with this, Mr McIver' he blustered as he was helped to his feet by one of the plod and manoeuvred towards the door.

McIver, a huge grin on his face, actually had the gall to nod to me as he passed by. 'Thanks, Nicker' he said.

'What was all that about?' Maurice was looking at me his face a picture of puzzlement. For me though, the penny had dropped with a vengeance.

'Do you fancy a month or three in Cornwall, or somewhere a long way off'? I asked him glumly. Mo looked even more puzzled.

'Nicker – they've just pulled Armlock and Charlie Griffin, so that leaves us free to go for the Stone, don't it?

I always tried to be patient with my pal, who was a bit slow at the best of times.

'Mate, they won't be able to touch Armlock for that job. In face I bet he will be back here within the hour – and looking for us if I am not very much mistaken. McIver has done us up like a pair of kippers Mo.'

'How?'

'Look, Charlie Griffin did that Hampstead job and will get done for it. Without Charlie's fingers Armlock won't be able to go for the Stone either. Trouble is that thanks to what McIver said, he now thinks that you and me, Maurice, were the ones who grassed him and Charlie up'. MoMo grinned nervously.

'Yeah, but Armlock knows we ain't grasses. Once we tell him why we was down the Nick he'll be alright, won't he'? Suddenly Mo wasn't so confident as he was trying to sound, and I had to explain further.

'Maurice – think about it mate. If you hadn't seen it with your own eyes would you believe McIver would have ever invited us down to open a safe in the nick so he could get his old woman's

- 97 -

present out of it – a little gift which just happened to be the one nicked in the Hampstead job by the way.

'And what was that little 'thank you Nicker' as he left? The git wanted Armlock to know how helpful we'd been to him', I added.

Finally the penny dropped and my mates face lit up with awareness, before immediately falling again as he realised the position.

'Yeah, Armlock can't go for the Stone without Charlie to open the doors for him and we can't, because we can't hang around here for a while. Stone me, Nicker, its like you said, McIver's done us up like kippers.'

I grinned, almost admiringly as I stood up. 'Yes – he's killed off two birds with one Hampstead stone. You ever done any sea-fishing, Maurice?'

14

Dagenham Posted

The Mild Bunch

I suppose we all had them – childhood friends, mates, pals, 'a gang'. I had the 'two Leslies', and I don't mean the old music hall act of Leslie Sarony and Leslie King whose biggest 'hit' was a song called 'Suzannah the sow'.

There were others – like Billy Bowden and Eric Johnson – but Leslie (Ginger) Barratt, and Leslie (known for more obscure reasons as 'Buddy') Blythe were the two other main scallywags of 'the Mild Bunch' – the scourge of Becontree Avenue in the forties.

Between watching the RAF having a pop at the Luftwaffe over our heads, swapping American comics and hunting for shrapnel, we played street soccer, park cricket, conkers and cigarette cards. Then as teenagers in the fifties, we boozed, bopped and were banned from the Ilford Palais before finally being broken up as we went out different ways to do our National Service. Ginger went into the army, Buddy into the RAF and I vanished into a couple of navies. (Royal and Merchant).

As kids we lived life to the full – well, as full as it could get in times when everyone was skint, our food came out of ration books, and our socks were darned instead of dumped. We nicked cheap water pistols out of Woolworth's to run amok, in our short trousers with hanging underpants and half-mast socks, among the bombsites squirting anyone in range with puddle water.

Ginger got me a real good hiding once – after we'd dawdled our way to Stevens Road Infant School one morning. The gate was shut when we go there, so we went home and were playing hopscotch in the street when my father arrived home for a mid-morning break from driving buses, and demanded an explanation.

Glibly I explained that the school was shut that day, but impetuously he grabbed me by the collar and marched me to the school to check it out. Needless to say the headmistress was more than happy to mark me off her register, and then humiliate me as a corner decoration in front of the class till dinnertime. Then, when I got home, I got a whacking from Mum while Ginger, whose parents never knew, got away with it.

As teenagers during the fifties, we had a ball – well, at least until the government invited us to learn how to kill Russian and Chinese communists. We'd started work, so we had money in our skies (sky rockets – pockets) that we hadn't had to sponge from dads, or earn by getting up in the early hours to deliver papers and / or milk or even nicking beer bottles to cash in for the deposits.

We went to Mr Doughty's dancing school in Heathway, so we could trawl for talent at the Saturday Night Hops in the Broad Street (Dagenham), and the Ilford, Baths, Seven Kings Library and the Palais. (Often dancing to the music of a local band led by a bloke called Kenny Ball – I often wonder whatever happened to him).

Buddy and I once went to a holiday camp – the one in Dovercourt later used in the Hi-Di-Hi sit-com. We spent seven days getting sloshed on Double Diamond, beaten at table tennis and snooker by little kids, and missing out on the talent because by the time we'd drunk enough Dutch courage, it was all spoken for.

Looking back on our teenage years, they really were full of life. We laughed at Max Miller at the East Ham Palace and Bob Hope at the Palladium, and we rock 'n' rolled to Presley and Bill Haley. We chain-smoked Woodbines out of chromium-plated cigarette cases as we cluttered up the Black and White Milk Bar drinking frothy coffee at weekends.

We often queued three times a week outside the Regent (Odeon) in Green Lane, the 'Mayfair' (ABC) in Becontree Heath and the Gaumont in Chadwell Heath, to see Gary Cooper, Johnny Weissmuller and Kirk Douglas or lust over Marilyn Monroe.

Our finest moment? Probably letting down the tyres on PC Lusher's bike and then going up on our toes. He'd left it outside a house in the Avenue while he was inside alleging we'd broken his front room window with a hand-carved boomerang that hadn't worked. He couldn't prove a thing – but he was right because I'd made it at work, thrown it and it hadn't come back.

Well, I was an engineering apprentice, not a carpenter. Anyway it made up for all the grief he'd given the Mild Bunch as kids.

15

Dagenham Posted

Scouting for urchins

A few years ago I kept a promise I made as I sat cross-legged on the floor in Lymington Road (Dagenham) school hall over half a century ago – I went back to Gilwell, and ran into a bunch of school-kids from Dagenham there on a visit.

In his book Scouting for Boys, Baden-Powell (BP) urged us to take cold baths if ever we harboured any 'libidinous thoughts'. To be honest, we wouldn't have known a libidinous thought from a dog biscuit at the time – but our eyes gleamed at the idea of camping out under the stars, and baking hedgehogs in clay in the embers of a campfire.

That was why I joined the 11th Dagenham – well that, and the glamour of the uniform. Bush hat (aka the Mounties), khaki shirt and shorts, and green neck-scarf held in position with a leather 'woggle' (never did learn to make a 'Turks Head' woggle). In our eyes it was the stuff of the backwoodsman, though I have to admit that in those 'hand me down' days of the forties my first Scout shirt had previously seen service as cousin Joan's Brownie's dress before being converted on Mum's sewing machine.

I'd progressed into the Scouts after a year or so as a Wolf Cub with the 11th, at a time of great post-war national jingoism. Life then was a constant display of enthusiasm for events like Empire

Day, and of course Armistice Day (Nov 11th), when we marched through the streets on church parades, sometimes behind a Boys Brigade band.

Youth was on the march in a way it doesn't seem to be today – as cubs we'd 'DYB DYB DYB'd (Do Your Best) our pledges to Akela, learned how to make telephone calls from public phone boxes and how to tell a reef knot from a bowline. As Scouts we carried sheath knives for effect, as much as for whittling and cutting wood, and poshed up their leather sheaths so they would look all Kit Carsonish and frontiersman on our belts. Though we didn't always appreciate it, it was a great time to be British, young and free of the war.

Camping was the real attraction though – and Gilwell Park, BP's old home near Chingford, the favoured venue. For ragamuffins whose only holiday was an occasional day trip to Southend, Gilwell was a promised land, a paradise for free spirits. Even before our first camp we'd sung around a mock camp-fire in Lymington Road's school hall about 'going back to Gilwell, happy land', as well as that traditional East End Zulu folk song, Ging Gang Gooley.

I swear Mum was a bit misty-eyed as she helped pack the rucksack we'd bought from the Army and Navy Stores in Green Lane, for that first camp. Old army blanket and groundsheet, along with change of clothes, knife, fork, spoon and 'two mugs – one for drinking out of', were all rammed into the rucksack, taking care to ensure the blanket was where it would be comfortable on my back, and I would not have a mug sticking into it as we walked.

We slept in wartime ex-army bivouac tents, on the sides of which we would leave our hats overnight to flatten out the brims and harden them with the dew. Some Scout Troops slept in bell tents – all coloured brown of course because they were also ex army – while others possessed big dirty white square tents like marquees. Gilwell Park today is a palette of brilliantly coloured tents huddled in little groups around its fields, but just after the war the shops making real money were the army surplus ones like the Army and Navy Stores. In them you could buy anything from tents to teaspoons – mess tins, blankets, boots, and rucksacks – you name it the Army and Navy had it all in abundance. For potential scouts it was a happy hunting ground where pennies really did mean something.

As Scouts we really did learn woodcraft, how to make campfires, cook bacon in ex-army (of course) mess-tins and brew tea (from tealeaves) in billycans perched somewhat precariously over the flames. We dined on tinned stews, peas (our biggest asset was a tin opener) and packets of dried potato some of it still on ration and which had to be brought from home. In camp it was all pooled, and our taste buds had new 'smoky flavoured' experiences then – wonderful gourmet, to us, moments that have never really been repeated, even in barbeques.

We built rope bridges between trees, learned survival techniques that might come in useful if ever we had to escape across Germany to the Swiss border, and we played football and cricket against Scouts from Liverpool, Newcastle and Manchester.

Perhaps the best time of all though was in the evening when hundreds of us left our camps to make our way down to the huge camp-fire to sing our little hearts out. There we disturb the night owls and keep all the other nocturnal animals on their toes, singing and ging,gang,gooley-ing in a variety of accents, without a libidinous thought between us.

Though there might have been a few er, funny Scoutmasters, of course.

Bob a Job on deposit

I don't know if they still do it, but in my 11th Dagenham heyday the Boy Scouts had a national fundraising week called ' Bob a Job' week. For seven days scouts all over the UK would take on any chores in the neighbourhood, based on a shilling (a bob) minimum a time.

The money was then collected and most of it sent on to national headquarters to help keep the movement going. If they still do it, it's probably a 'Quid a Bid' now with people bidding a quid to have a job done – at least I hope so.

Now some people did take liberties, and I remember a woman not far from where we lived in particular. She actually got me, and some members of my patrol I'd brought in to help do the job, to dig her garden over. It took a couple of days of really hard graft, and at the end of it she gave us...a shilling between us. Believe me it took a great deal of restraint, and obedience to the Scout Law, to stop us going back there one night and tipping a few dustbins over her front garden.

In fairness most people gave us more than the required shilling – occasionally even extra on the side for ourselves. The garden episode had left our donations forms looking a little sparse despite all our hard work over several days, and we were desperate. So we did something Baden Powell would have de-woggled us for, and he would certainly have taken my Patrol Leader's stripes away.

We were coming back down the Avenue, disgusted but as true scouts bearing it in good grace, when we passed the off licence that stood in the parade of shops where Becontree Avenue and Valence Avenue meet. In my day it was called Clifford's Corner on account of the big drapery store there. As we reached the 'offie' a couple of kids walked into it with some empty bottles in their hands, clearly taking them in to get their deposits back. It was one of those 'Be Prepared' moments, when leadership initiative blossomed over desperation.

I beckoned my little bunch of stalwarts and we went round the back of the shops, where a small service road backed onto them on that side, and where I'd remembered something else. That off licence had a small yard at the back for deliveries and collections, and which had a very rickety fence and an even less stable gate on it.

It was padlocked but peering through the gaps we could see lots and lots of lovely bottle crates stacked up against that back fence, right near where the gateway was. Yeah, you've guessed it – within seconds we had hands pushing through the gaps in that fence, widening it sufficiently to liberate some of the bottles.

It wasn't actually as difficult as it sounds because, to be honest, the gate gaped at its bottom end by nearly a foot so a youthful 'scoutly' arm was well able to reach inside it to help ourselves to some booty. Then, armed with about a dozen of the bottles we'd nicked from its yard, we went into the off licence to reclaim the money. We explained that we'd collected the bottles from our dads so we could use the deposit money for scout funds. No problem, and the money was handed over without question.

In fact it was so easy that every Wednesday (Scout night) for weeks I went back to that gaping gate to see what I could bottles I could liberate, and reclaim the money on. It had to be Scout night of course, because the offie manager would never question the morality and integrity of a Boy Scout in uniform. Not that it was going into scout funds after that first 'raid' of course.

Nor were the 'redeemed deposits' gained from similar attacks on vulnerable pubs, off licences and clubs like the Winding Way Social Club near us. In fact in the months to come, once I involved the Mild Bunch as well, anywhere fences could be scaled or gates forced open for feverish fingers to grab empty Mann & Crossman Brown Ale and Mackeson Stout bottles were fair game.

It was certainly a bit safer than organising distractions in Woolworths so we could nick cheap toys or bottles of scent, from their open counters as the assistants looked elsewhere. That, in any case, would have been stealing and thus against the Scout Law – when we had the bottles away, we were returning them after all – not nicking them.

Today's Scout Law after all, says: '**A Scout makes good use of time and is careful of possessions and property'**. We were making good use of our time, and we were being careful of possessions and property. Ok, strictly speaking they weren't our possessions and property, but one out of three ain't bad!

16

VIEWPOINT

The lips move!

One of the oldest jokes about politicians ever is that you can tell when they are lying, because their lips move. Believe me, many a true word said in jest – and I know because I was once a politician, well of sorts and rubbed shoulders with a lot of them.

Back in the early seventies I was persuaded to join the Pilgrims Hatch branch of the Brentwood Labour Party ultimately in 1974 I stood for, and was elected to, Brentwood District Council. I was one of eleven Labour members that were, in the following May elections, reduced to four – me and three others.

I had also developed a natural skill for exploiting publicity for the party and the Pilgrims Hatch Labour Party had actually become quite a force in the local scheme of socialist thinking. We ran socials and other events for the Hatch's old people and generally kept ourselves busy on the town political front. To be honest I was not the best kind of councillor because while I am pretty eloquent tapping out the finger words on a keyboard, I was always less active with the tongue and tonsils in the council chamber.

I wasn't completely silent but we did have some 'mouthy' members among our four and I was happy to let them get on with it. I had also discovered an alarming tendency to disagree with some of the 'comrades', who seemed to think and say whatever the party line said they could think and say.

In addition I had committed the ultimate sin by even developing some friendships on the Tory bench, particularly with a certain Tony Donnelly. He, along with a Mike Gibson, had actually won two of the Pilgrims Hatch seats in May, making me the sole Labour Pilgrims Hatch voice on the council.

God forgive me I had even formed a great friendship with our Tory MP Robert McCrindle who really did become a great friend, and remained so until his sad death many years later. A thoroughly decent and honest politician he was knighted before having to stand down because of the cancer, which later killed him.

So there were already mutterings against me for such 'treachery' among some of the more leftward leaning comrades especially after I had dared to be seen actually having a pint or two with the likes of Tony D. He is also a lifelong friend to this day and in the past we have actually done some business together.

It all really fell apart in 1976 when Harold Wilson's (another man for whom truth was not essential) Labour government brought in the Race Relations Act. Aimed at forcing racial equality, it was in my view, and remains, it was one of the daftest pieces of legislation ever to pass through Parliament, because it sought to instruct and enforce, rather than persuade.

I have always argued that the best people to bring about a natural integration in race relations were sports and show business personalities. We had cheered on black British fighters like Randolph Turpin, athletes and footballers like Pele for years. We had been entertained by the voice of Shirley Bassey, and applauded the performances of entertainers like Kenny Lynch (no relation) and actors of the calibre of Sydney Poitier, without noticing they were black. We did not need to be ordered to treat them as equals – they were doing that themselves, gaining respect for their achievements.

I remember in the 1990s when I was doing some promotion work for the Endeavour special needs school in Brentwood, I asked Frank Bruno (who lived locally) to come and see us. The kids, all white as it happens, were all over him. They never saw a black man – just a great familiar face and laugh they'd seen on the telly, and in my view Frank is one of the greatest weapons the cause for racial equality has.

But in 1976 if you were a Labour member, you were not allowed to hold such public views – though many of our local politicians in the party were equally doubtful of the Act in private. So when I had a letter published in the Brentwood Gazette calling for the repeal of the Race Relations Act, only weeks after it had been passed into law, the local heavens opened up and fell upon me.

What seemed to upset many of my 'comrades' was that I had signed the letter as 'Cllr Brian Lynch'. Well, I say upset – it infuriated them and they demanded I be called to account on that alone, saying I was a Labour councillor and had brought the party into disrepute with my 'racist' outburst.

I appeared before a local Labour Party 'kangaroo court' who demanded I explain my actions and my views. I told my 'judges', who were never prepared to listen anyway, of my own theories about natural integration. I certainly denied being racist and still do to this day. I also pointed out to them that I had been elected as a Brentwood Councillor who happened to be a Labour Party member, and that if I wanted to I would sign cheques with the title.

I went on to point out that if they wanted to persecute me further I would resign from the party and from the council – a threat which brought about a lot of laughs from people saying that politicians never resigned their seats. So the next day I resigned.

I did get an invite, before the resignation went public, to cross the floor and join the Tory lot, but there was no way I could do that. In any case I had already been talking to the editor of the (now defunct) Brentwood Argus about doing some freelance work for him and covering the council for the paper. I hadn't felt obliged to tell my Labour tormentors that, but I never lied to them about it either.

That is what I did, and was from then on ostracised by the 'comrades' and in the resulting by-election they lost the seat.

Now, thirty years later, I see Labour government ministers actually saying that to say such things as I was arguing then wasn't racist after all. Of course a few years ago when the then Tory leader Michael Howard was calling for a look at race relations, he was immediately castigated as being racist by the same people who now say we were both right.

So do politicians lie, or speak with forked tongues, as a matter of course? Clearly not all of them, but how many people now believe every word that comes out of Tony Blair's mouth for example? In 1945 Clement Attlee's Labour government brought us the NHS and the welfare state. Blair's has brought us war, gambling casinos and 24-hour boozing that is already causing the NHS some problems.

At least Clem Attlee wasn't lying about his beliefs – any more than Thatcher was come to that – but Blair? Just watch his lips!

17

Dagenham Posted

Power corrupts? Yeah, so?

I have never been one to shirk responsibility, and my life has brought me into many positions of power. I've been an editor and departmental head, naval officer (Merchant), Scout patrol leader, football team captain and even shop steward and FOC (Father of the Chapel in newspapers), at various times during my three-score years and more.

Real power though, lies in the ability not to just lead but to control a supply, and I guess the most personally rewarding experience I had of that, was when I was doing my national service in the Royal Navy. In those days we had a daily rum ration just before lunch, and when we were in barracks it had to be collected by someone from each mess, or hut, who was unofficially designated the 'rum bosun'.

Usually that was the leading hand, but often at weekends or if he was away anyone could collect it and there was usually a bit of a rush to volunteer – something of a rarity in the navy as I recall. The reason was simple – there always more rum in the container than there were blokes to drink it, which meant there was some over to be shared around by anyone else – i.e. the 'rum rats' who always hovered around at tot time. One reason there was always rum over was because when you doled each tot out in its metal measuring cup, you always kept your thumb in it so as to make sure a full ration was never really served up. There was also the fact that some guys went ashore before tot time, so they still had their tot allocated by the 'pusser' (purser).

If you never took the rum ration – and incredibly some didn't – you qualified for sixpence a day extra. Even then that wasn't a lot, but the real value in taking it lay in its marketability. You'd be surprised what favours you could get for a sip (sippers) gulpers (a mouthful) or even the whole tot. A week's gulpers for example could get you off an unwanted watch duty, and you could get all your laundry done for a week's tot if someone was a defaulter on punishment and denied their own official rum ration as a result.

I ought to explain that a tot, for those in a shore base, was based on two to one – two of water to one of navy rum, so it almost filled a small tumbler. At sea you could claim the rum neat, and on the one occasion I did that I regretted it immediately because it was thick and so powerful it resulted in me fighting to get my breath back.

Normally, it was doled out by the purser supervised by the Officer of the Watch and the Master at Arms. The rum bosun would claim for the members present in the mess, a figure that would be checked off by the purser, who would then pour sufficient rum for the mess allocation into the container to be carried away to the mess deck.

In fact qualifying for your tot was like cash in hand – being rum bosun (and tradition had it that he always got sippers from everyone) was a real power bonus. It was something I managed to achieve several times at HMS Hornet (the Motor Torpedo Boats base in Gosport). It was not, however my first experience of power and what it can achieve.

It had been a heady climb in fact, which can be traced back to the moment I was handed my first badge of authority – as the ink monitor in Stevens Road Junior School – though there was no actual badge with that job.

Today we live in the wonderful world of the Bic, where hasty scribble is king and the well-formed hand that 'proper ink' encouraged is a rarity. Even Biro, the inventor of the ball pen, is barely acknowledged as the man who put the skids under the ink monitor.

Yet it was a milestone. We'd left the infant school with its chalk, crayons and plasticine to move into proper desks, with lids, long slots for pencils and pens, and neat round holes for china inkwells. They arrived gleaming and fresh from the caretaker's office, having been scrubbed clean by his wife during the summer holidays.

We were handed wooden penholders and gold coloured nibs, before being lectured on how to behave with the old blue/black. 'Your mothers will not appreciate having to clean ink from your handkerchiefs, or from shirts which have been hit from behind with pellets of paper soaked in ink. So you do not mess around with it...do I make myself clear?'

Having delivered her warning her eye fell upon me. 'Lynch, you will take yourself down to the caretaker's room and ask him for ink. You will be ink monitor and it will be your responsibility to make sure all the inkwells are filled whenever they need to be.'

Wow! This was clearly the big time, and my rise to glory had begun – though I confess I was never trusted with the half sheets of blotting paper they gave us every term. (Well it was wartime, after all). In fact, it was quite amazing that the government found enough metal left over from making shells and Spitfires to ensure the schools had sufficient pen-nibs.

Certainly we found them very useful, because a touch of heavy pressure on the tip snapped it, leaving two very sharp points. It didn't take long to find a way of attaching small paper flights to them, and we had darts able to inflict a fair amount of pain on an unsuspecting neck.

Nor did it take my classmates long to realise that the quickest way to empty an inkwell was not to dip a pen in it, but a lump of chalk. I tell you, some days I had more wells on the go than a Dallas oilman. Of course no one uses them any more, and the days when the silence of an examination room would be broken by the rhythmic scratching of fifty pen nibs on paper are long gone.

Then the fountain pens arrived. True they were in before the war and were very expensive but they got cheaper, and you could fill their rubber storage sacs with ink by lifting a lever on its side. You could also empty it at speed, and distance, onto a collar in front by the same lever. The unlucky shirt wearer never knew about it until his mum whacked him when he got home. Lot more painless than a pointed dart, and much easier to disclaim responsibility for.

I held that job as ink monitor for my first term in Stevens Road Junior, but I had clearly impressed because for the next term I was appointed as the class milk monitor. Now this was real power! My new duties were to go and collect the crates of free milk we kids drank in the classroom before lunch, but between the collection point and the classroom was the boy's cloakroom.

In that room hung the usual assortment of hand-me-down overcoats, and some of us also used to hang haversacks into which doting mums had placed our lunchtime Spam or fish paste sandwiches. There was plenty of room in them for about four or five of the small (one third of a pint) bottles of milk to be stowed away en route to the classroom because nobody ever checked the number of bottles. We just got a couple of crates, depending on how many usually in the class, and any left over went into the staff room for their tea, I guess.

There were occasions when I swapped the odd bottle of milk for a hundred cigarette cards or a dozen marbles, but mostly they helped supplement Mum's United Dairies daily doorstep delivery. Well, in those days every little helped. Along with the milk monitor's job I got a little lapel 'Monitor' badge to proudly wear to show my authority. Never got that as an ink distributor, and in neither job did we tend to nod off in the afternoons.

The rum rats, on the other hand, did!

18

STORY

The other man's grass is always greener

'Lambert, I don't feel I need to suggest you keep schtumm about this, do I?' The menace in Armlock's voice was pretty unmistakeable, as was the close proximity to my nose of his rather beefy friends. Hastily I reassured him that the three wise monkeys were right little chatterboxes, compared with MoMo and me.

'Oh, come on Harry. You know us better than that. We've had our differences over the years, but we are not grasses and you know it' I told him. I breathed an inward sigh of relief as his apes took the pressure off my nasal functions by moving downwind at his gesture to back off.

His podgy face suddenly opened up into a broad grin, and he signalled for another couple of pints to be brought over to our table. 'Good lads! I knew I could rely on a couple of old pals'; he laughed, before moving away to the table he always occupied when he was taking up his collections.

Well, when I say collections I don't mean to imply there were any charity boxes involved. The kind of collection Armlock Harry Foster went in for were more in the nature of insurance premiums, handed over by local shopkeepers and landlords to ensure their premises remained intact for another week or two, than charity donations.

It was certainly a more lucrative and less onerous way of life than the one he'd led in his younger days when he wrestled (hence the nickname) for a living. That was until he'd been recruited to mind a local villain called Jackie Roberts. Then, when Roberts had mysteriously vanished, some say into a flyover support, Armlock had taken over the business. Astonishingly, he'd gone on to show he had brains as well as brawn, by doing rather well at it. These days, as well as the lucrative insurance premiums paid by the kosher businesses, most of the local scallywags also found it wiser to pay Armlock a 'licence fee' if they wanted to nick anything on the manor. Even if the job meant playing away, they knew better than not to invite Armlock to send in some troops to help out for a percentage in lieu of keeping them safe from harm afterwards.

Mind you, it had always irritated him that his old school chums Nicker Lambert and Maurice Morris (MoMo) had kept him at arms length as far as that went. While we retained a healthy respect for him, and his thugs, we generally kept ourselves to ourselves as independent operators, because we had brains and brawn too. Well, in a manner of speaking we did. On the occasion we did interfere somewhat with one of his jobs, we got a right pasting as a result.

MoMo is a big lad with muscles and fists like footballs, but a bit short on thinking capacity, while I had the brains that usually kept us out of trouble along with one or two other skills. Having said that, it was also well known on the manor that we had some scores to settle with Armlock, and suddenly, that morning, the gods had smiled upon us.

We'd been sitting quietly in the White Horse, drinking what was left of some ill-appropriated gains, when a well-dressed figure with a vaguely familiar face had pushed the doors of the pub open. He'd looked hurriedly around the pub before spotting us and scurrying over to our table.

'Give this to Armlock!' he'd gasped, thrusting a large brown envelope into my hand before dashing over to the bar, and tried to look as if he'd been there since opening time.

He hardly reached it before a couple more bodies pushed the doors open – and while they weren't wearing uniforms it was pretty obvious to the trained eye that they were local plod. They had a quick squint around, and then made straight over to the geezer, and within seconds he was grabbed, read some alleged rights and marched back out again wearing a pair of coppers bracelets. I mean, a bloke can't even have a quiet drink these days without the bizzies cluttering the place up. It was all over in a matter of a minute or so, and once they'd gone the pub was immediately back to normal as if nothing had happened.

MoMo and I sat there for a few moments looking at the mysterious envelope, and wondering what it had all been about. Unusually, it was MoMo who woke up first.

'Nicker, did you see who that was? Don't you remember 'im?'

I shook my head, knowing I ought to have recognised the flying postman, but couldn't place him. MoMo had copped him though and suddenly got quite excited.

'It was Charlie Jensen. Remember? We turned him over on that wage snatch fiddle.'

That's when the penny dropped – MoMo was right, and for once way ahead of me. Remember him? Boy, did we owe that guy! We'd thought we'd been clever, nicking a payroll before Armlock's team had carried out their own blagging for it, but Jensen had shopped us and not to the Old Bill either.

The bloke we'd thought was just the firm's chief cashier turned out to be Armlock's inside man, and he'd fingered us to him. MoMo and I had got a right smacking and lost the dosh. Neither of us had ever forgotten those bruises, or how much we owed Armlock and Jensen, so I was a bit surprised that Mo had clocked him before I did.

Obviously the geezer had been in such a panic to get shot of the envelope before the rozzers who'd been chasing him had arrived, he'd not recognised us either, as anyone other than as familiar faces who were probably on Armlock's team. The envelope he'd left in our 'safe keeping' wasn't sealed so, just to ensure it really was safe and sound of course, I opened it. I pulled out the sheet of paper inside it, and MoMo peered over my shoulder and we examined it, with growing interest, because it was right up our street.

It was a plan of a building, but what really drew our eye was the word 'safe' indicated by a cross in one of the rooms, along with some figures that did seem they might just be the combination to the safe. There were other marks that we knew from long experience in these things represented the presence of pressure and beam 'alarms' in various other places in and around the building. It never took either of us long to realise what we were looking at – opportunity!

All we had to do was actually identify the premises so thoughtfully marked out for us, and that had taken us less than a minute or so. It was the same Aztec Engineering Company in Romford – whose wage packets we'd turned over before, and where Jensen was apparently still the Chief Cashier.

Seconds after we'd realised it, Armlock himself had swept into the pub with his team, so I'd hurriedly memorised it, sealed the envelope and called him over to hand it over to him. His eyes had narrowed as he'd torn it open and read what was inside. Then they flickered back to us again.

'Have you read this, Nicker?' he glared.

'Never had the chance Harry mate. He just dashed in and out again, and in any case it's still sealed.'

I lied through my back teeth of course, while I grinned at him with the front ones. That was when he'd gone into his sweetness and light 'old pals' routine, before stuffing the envelope into his pocket. Then he'd left us to drink his beer while he went over to do his coin collecting – not that coins were much in evidence as far as we could see.

MoMo and I sat looking at each other – both with the same thought in mind. Well two thoughts really – how to get our hands on what was in that safe, and how to do it before Armlock did. We'd never actually mentioned why Jensen had been in such a hurry, or any little extra details like the couple of coppers who'd helped him out the door, so Armlock had no reason to hold off doing the joint, as he'd originally planned.

The problem was that he'd already caught us out over the first con we'd pulled in the Aztec offices, and Armlock was no fool. Given the circumstances about the envelope, along with the coincidence of it being about the same source we were proposing to liberate the dosh from, we were clearly setting

Still In My Own Lynchtime

ourselves up for another session with the cricket-stumps. (Armlock was very patriotic when it came to sporting weaponry, and dead against baseball bats on principle.)

MoMo broke the silence first. 'What do you think, Nicker? Are we going after this or not?' he muttered, obviously not desperately anxious to be overheard from the other side of the room. I took another large swig out of the glass, before replying.

'Oh yeah Mo. We owe Armlock that much at least, don't we! Anyway we've got a score to settle with him as well', I grinned. 'Come on, let's go!'

Well, not to put too fine a point on it, when Armlock sent a team into the Aztec offices that night, they found the Bill sitting comfortably in the dark waiting for them. Before they could say, 'It's a fair cop, guv', they were in the back of some blues and twos on their way to Market Street and a chat with Neil McIver, Chief Inspector of this parish.

All very sad, really – well, it's always the way when someone has been grassed up and had their collar felt. Everyone was talking about it in the White Horse later that night, where Armlock was having some long and serious chat with his bent briefs in the corner. We acted all sympathetic of course, and while some nasty suspicions might have crossed his mind at first, the fact that we were there was clear evidence that McIver's information hadn't come from us.

Indeed from what we could hear, Armlock was cursing Jensen, and snarling that he'd had clearly sung like a canary. He was pledging some pretty dire consequences when Jensen, who he knew by then had been nicked the previous day, next appeared in his sights. It was pretty clear that Charlie boy was no longer on Armlock's Christmas card list.

Indeed Armlock even let us buy him a whisky chaser as we commiserated with him, though we never liked to mention it had been paid for with former Aztec money of course. It gave me a good excuse to sour Jensen's pitch even further.

'Now you come to mention it Harry, that must have been why he dashed in here in such a hurry with that envelope yesterday. Yeah, come to think of it, he did leave with a pair of plod holding his arms', I recalled.

Well, as things turned out Armlock's team got sent down for breaking and entering as well as suspicion of conspiracy to rob. Jensen of course was released without charge, because he was in custody when Armlock's lot arrived on the scene, but promptly went up on his toes. He'd got the message that his 'friendship' with Armlock was now on pretty thin ice, and the fortunate discovery of a one-way Easyjet ticket to Rumania on his doormat when he got home, had convinced him it was time to vanish.

It was actually pretty nice of Armlock to send him the ticket as a hint to start travelling. Well, it would have been if Harry had sent it himself! In fact it was MoMo and I who'd dropped it through his letterbox. Well, why not? We could afford it and it helped make Jensen look as though he was the grass.

When we'd turned Jensen over the first time, it had been with the help of some almost genuine police warrant cards. MoMo had once picked them up under circumstances I would sooner not go into at this stage, and as it happened we still had them. So, after we left the White Horse that afternoon we'd nipped back to my pad to pick them up. I also stuck a DIY search warrant I knocked up on the computer in a couple of minutes in my bin before we left for Romford.

When we got to the Aztec Engineering Company's chief cashier's office, I introduced myself to his secretary as Chief Inspector McIver, and MoMo as my sergeant. Fortunately it was a different girl from the last one Jensen had had and she was clearly wondering where her boss had got to that afternoon. Flashing the snide search warrant I told her that he was under arrest and that I intended to search his office. Scared the life out of her.

I ordered her not to move, or make any phone calls that might implicate her, because my 'sergeant' would stay in the outer office with her to ensure she made no such moves while I searched her bosses' office. It only took me a few minutes to open that safe – a skill I'd picked up many years before, but knowing the combination anyway helped of course – and remove the contents.

Then I'd come out of the office and told her I had found nothing so far, but that the whole place was now a crime scene.

Still In My Own Lynchtime

She could go, after leaving her name and address with 'Sergeant MoMo', but I wanted her to come down to the Market Street police station that afternoon with a solicitor to make a statement.

She couldn't get out of the place quick enough and, once she'd clattered down the corridor and out into the warm afternoon sunshine, we locked up for her and did a runner.

By the time Armlock's lot turned up that evening the safe was already about £10K lighter than it had been, but the rozzers had never had reason to check it out anyway. Well, not until the girl had turned up at the nick with her story and solicitor of course.

The following day they released Jensen for lack of evidence, telling him that they had arrested and charged the burglars with breaking and entering and wanted a statement from him. He knew straight off that no one would ever believe that he hadn't grassed Armlock, and the discovery of the no-frills airline ticket to Dracula-land would have seemed very welcome hint that a change of scenery could go a long way to saving his legs. He'd dashed off to Stansted like a frightened rabbit.

I'd had gambled that McIver, who obviously had his suspicions, would set his trap at the Aztec that night thinking that the two imitation coppers who'd frightened the girl had been casing the place that afternoon. He obviously wouldn't let Jensen go until he had the burglars that he'd suspected would turn up either.

Who was it, who said that the other man's grass was always greener?

19

Dagenham Posted

Whatever happened to 'Nipper'?

We had three parks within easy reach of the Avenue – well Barking might have been a bit of a walk, but Goodmayes and Valence were well within trotting distance while Barking had its boating and tiddler-fishing lake.

Goodmayes was run by Ilford council and had very strict guidelines about what you could play there – it had to be cricket in the summer and football in the winter. Socialist Dagenham, on the other hand, ran Valence Park, and you could play football there at any time of the year.

I went back there recently – the swimming pool has gone, along with the sandpit and paddling pool, but our Wembley Stadium pitches were still there. It was to them that, with or without a ball, we would go with our football boots strung around our necks and jackets ready to become goalposts.

We didn't need a ball because there was always a small gang of kids over the park somewhere and always up for a challenge match. On the occasions we had a ball we were approached ourselves, whatever park we were in, by a bunch of lads looking for a game. Such challenges were never refused.

So it was that we played, without really knowing it, against the likes of Jimmy Graves, who lived between Valence and Parsloes Park and possibly even young Bobby Moore in Barking.

Still In My Own Lynchtime

I like to think that the fat kid I once skipped past, leaving him floundering as I did my Stanley Matthews bit, was the guy I later came to idolise as West Ham's golden boy.

The fact was that these were not just parks – they were our Upton Parks, Stamford Bridges and Highburys as much as our Wembley Stadiums. For hour upon hour, whatever the weather, we would hone our footballing skills on their hallowed turfs (and our cricketing ones on the Lords that Goodmayes Park stood in for on a summers day).

There would be rumours that 'scouts' from all the big clubs would be sitting on park benches, watching us kicking the living daylights out of someone one else's shin pads. I mean, by and large we played fair and seldom argued over whether a ball was over a non-existent crossbar or not, but we took no prisoners either.

These were games played with leather panelled footballs laced up with leather laces. In wet weather they could break your foot if you hit them wrong and one reason why few of us liked 'rising up like Tommy Lawton' to head the ball was that if it was the lace part that connected with your head, you knew it. Inside right Stanley Mortenson once joked that the reason he liked playing with Matthews was because Stan could cross the ball onto your head with the lace facing outwards away from the head.

But in fairness we did have some memorable, and very sporting, games over Valence Park especially, and never refused a request from another kid for a game. I remember one in particular when Ginger Barratt, Buddy Blythe and I agreed to let a little kid a few years younger than us but who lived round the corner in Bonham Road have a kickabout game.

I remember it because us fit and active young teenagers would flop down when the ball was kicked too hard and flew half a mile up the other end of the park. We left it to the nipper who was full of energy (and tricks). He was dead keen and never flopped down exhausted with me and the lads – just ran after the ball and brought it back so we could start playing again. In fact we let him play with us any time he asked when we were over Valence Park, because he was so useful.

Yeah, I often wonder what happened to Nipper Venables.

20

Dagenham Posted

Somebody out there owes me a pony!

Back in the late fifties you couldn't move in pub car parks for beaten up old vans with names like *'Ebenezer Scrooge and the Misers'*, the *'Dominoes'* or the *'Hound Dogs'* badly painted on their sides. From Liverpool to Catford, bunches of scruffy young urchins were playing weekend gigs in old air raid shelters and pubs, before going back to the factory on Monday morning.

Dreaming of stardom the Scousers and the Cockney kids belted out rock'n roll and skiffle on second hand guitars or washing boards and oil drums. This was also an era when being 'cockney' was fashionable along with jellied eels and talking of 'monkeys' (£500) and 'ponys' (£25) was almost obligatory.

This new breed of alleged musicians were however, at least playing live music. A few years down the line and they'd be replaced by silver-tongued hippies with no talent above that of being able to rabbit, but who did own of a pile of gramophone records, a microphone and a set of very loud ear-splitting amplifiers.

About this time I came home after a few years in the Royal and Merchant navies to start work in what I still (to irritate Dearly Beloved), call the 'glue factory'. It was a firm in Manor Park that made wallpaper paste, and it was where I found her – and have been stuck with her ever since. (Sorry love – just joking – so put

Still In My Own Lynchtime

that rolling pin down!) We spent a year or so courting in pubs all over Ilford, Dagenham and Barking, before finally fixing 'the day', following a proposal, which is a story in itself.

Weddings were not so expensive as they appear to be now. My seamstress sister Pat made the wedding and bridesmaid dresses, we booked a school hall in Ripple Road for the reception, and found a cheap caterer to do the sit down ham salad for a few quid a head. Some uncles working in the docks provided the obligatory sherry for the toast.

We were getting married in St Margaret's in Barking that, because since it was where Captain Cook did the biz himself, seemed very right to me as an ex-seaman. It proved to be a windy but dry day and everything went like clockwork – well everything except the music that is.

About a year earlier, once Liz and I had set the wheels in motion, my mother happened to mention that the son of a friend of hers was part of a band. This was good because although, as I have said, these bands were sprouting all over the country at the time, they were in great demand in the pubs especially on Saturday nights. So it was necessary to get one booked sharpish, and we did.

Then, a few weeks before August 25th (which by the way happens to be Liberation Day in France) I decided to run a last minute check to make sure all was well. It was only then that we heard that the band, for which I had already paid a fiver deposit towards their £30 gig fee, had disbanded.

Clearly this was not good news, but the lady whose son had been part of the original band said he was still involved with a group, and they would do the date themselves. Huge sighs of relief all round.

Came the day and we went through the rituals. We had our sherry, lunch and speeches reception and then had a break for a couple of hours until the evening when we would be expecting the bulk of our guests for the evening booze-up.

My father and I took the chance to set up the bar in a small anteroom next to the main hall. We heard the band arrive, and once they had been paid the balance of the agreed fee in the shape of a pony (£25), they began to set up their kit in the main hall. Dad and I were just trying out the beer to see it was settled enough to be poured of course, when they started to strum up with the music and dancing.

It was just after that that we heard a few shouts, and my brother Roy came out into the 'bar' to suggest I came out because there was trouble brewing. I got out there to find that another band had arrived and the musicians were all squaring up to each other. Indeed a couple of drummers were threatening dire retribution upon each other with their drumsticks.

Clearly there had been something of a mix-up over bookings and eventually it turned out that the band that had just arrived really was ours. The first group had been booked for a wedding reception all right, but in a school hall further down Ripple Road. They went on their way and peace was restored – but I'd forgotten something until the other lot asked for their money.

So if a guitar-playing or drum bashing pensioner with a conscience, whose group was booked on to play in a wedding reception in Barking on August 25th 1962 but went to the wrong school first, reads this perhaps he would like to return my pony.

21

Dagenham Posted

The assassins

I read a letter in the Dagenham Post in which a lady complained about having suffered from mice in her house for months. It reminded me of my late father because, when it came to catching mice he could have taught that Pied Piper chappie a thing or three. He never used a flute, poison, or even traps – he used tins of beans.

Not that the old man was a natural born killer by any means. During the war every one kept rabbits and chickens both for their fur (as far as the rabbits went) and their eggs (chickens) as much as for the occasional meal supplementing the meagre meat ration. My mother had many a rabbit's pelt stretched out and salted as it dried out sufficiently to provide us with gloves, mittens, and even the occasional rug. Dad, you see, could kill rabbits without a qualm.

When it was their turn to make the ultimate sacrifice he had no compunction whatsoever about holding them up by their hind legs and whacking them on the back of the neck with the copper stick. I suppose I ought to explain in this 21st century that the copper used to stand in the scullery and was what we heated water up for baths or for mum's washing. The copper stick was a big thick lump of wood, which was used to help drag wet (and very hot) clothes out of the copper so they could be worked on with the scrubbing board. Scrubbing board? Work it out for yourself!

Anyway, as I said Dad sent many a backyard bred rabbit to bunny-heaven so that we could have a good Sunday lunch. Chickens though, presented him with a problem. The big burly guy who could whack a bunny into kingdom come, slit its throat for the blood to drain and then skin it like a fur trapper, could not kill a bird.

That usually involved gripping the shrieking chicken between the knees, gripping it by the neck and giving it a sharp and sudden twist to break its neck. Sometimes people did chop their heads off, giving rise to all the stories about headless chickens dashing down the garden. Dad couldn't do it – but he knew an uncle who could.

Uncle Frank, who lived a few streets away had no compunction about chicken neck wringing – but oddly enough he couldn't kill a rabbit to save his life. Dad and Uncle Frank made a good pair of assassins, provided each kept to his own victim. If we had a chicken nearing its eat-by date, Uncle Frank would arrive while if he had a taste for rabbit stew that weekend, Dad would pop round to Uncle Frank's with his copper stick. It all worked rather well actually, but in fairness there was a lot of killing going on at the time, with the Luftwaffe doing most of it.

We also had plenty of household pests then, along with the means to deal with them. We would eat with a sticky strip stuffed with corpses of ex-flies dangling above us, stink our clothes out with mothballs, and set nasty little traps for rats and mice. We also kept a tabby cat who, while he never knew the pleasures of modern cat food, did eat what we ate – or rather what we didn't eat.

Dad had a particular horror of mice – he wouldn't even let them use our air raid shelter during the blitz. He'd been raised in the slums of Wapping where people shared their poverty with the mice, rats, lice and cockroaches. Out here, in 'the Dagenham countryside', we didn't have the lice, but we did have the cockroaches, earwigs and ants making quick skirmishes into the scullery (which is what we called the kitchen before we

Still In My Own Lynchtime

got posh). We also had the mice – oh boy, did we have the mice despite the cat.

The oil-shop (they call them hardware stores these days) always did a roaring trade in mousetraps, flypapers and Harpic, along with packets of mysterious powders, crystals and bottles of liquid guaranteed to kill anything that flew, crawled or buzzed – even the kids. Eating our dinner while watching the flies and bluebottles struggling on the sticky strips dangling from the ceiling above us was our normal cabaret.

For some reason, mice were dad's particular abomination – he just couldn't stand them. In fact one reason we'd left East Ham one step ahead of the Luftwaffe, was because he'd come home from work one night, and looked into where his two young sons were sleeping, as fathers do. To his horror he found a mouse running across his eldest boy's (mine) face.

That had made up his mind that we had to get out to some decent housing, and we'd moved to the Becontree Estate as a result. Just as well really, because not long after we fled Telham Road the Luftwaffe reshaped it into a bombsite, so I guess in a way that errant mouse could well have saved all our lives.

We'd had a black cat to deal with the house livestock at first. Sadly he was so black he got caught in the front door during the blackout one night when his head was going through it just as Mum slammed it shut. Who said black cats were lucky? But, Dad's favourite mice-killing weapon was a tin of beans. Now, after all these years, I can pass on his secret to any other mouse tormented soul including that lady who wrote into the local paper.

First take your can of beans and open one end. Pour the beans into a saucepan and heat them up, while toasting a couple of slices of bread. Then enjoy beans on toast, preferably with a nice cup of tea, for breakfast.

Suitably refreshed, after breakfast take the empty bean tin and cut off the other end of the tin as well. The next step is to take the two ends and bend them to a rightangle. You now have two hinge-like shapes ready for action.

Find the hole in the skirting board where the little sod has chewed its way into the room, and then take a hammer and a few nails. Use them to nail one side of the 'hinge' to the floor and the other into the skirting board to cover the hole. I defy any mouse to chew its way through a Heinz tin.

In fact there's one house in the Avenue that to this day, could still have 57 variety reminders all round its front room – and I bet it still doesn't get any mice.

22

STORY

Dishonour among thieves

Willie Martin was surprised to see me alright. His little rat like eyes glittered with insincerity, but also looked a little worried as I sat down heavily and plonked my pint onto the table. I put a glass of Bells in front of him, and gestured to him to help himself.

'Hiya, Nicker!' His voice quavered nervously as he spoke. 'ows fings?'

I picked up my pint and took a good long pull of best bitter before answering. While I drank I stared at him, and that appeared to make him even more jittery just as I knew it would. Putting the glass down, I wiped my lips before sticking a cigarette between them and lighting it. I was making every moment as slow and deliberate as I could, before answering.

'Well. I suppose it depends on how you look at it Will', I finally replied.

To be honest – and in fairness, honesty has never been one of my greatest virtues – I'd been blazing mad when I'd found the Merc missing from the drive in front of our house. I'd started making enquiries through the manor – always more favourable than bringing the Old Bill in of course, but without real progress. Then, when the car had reappeared just as mysteriously a couple of days later, and I'd read the note stuck under the windscreen wiper, I'd started to feel a lot better.

'Dear Sir,' the note said. 'I really must apologise for having to borrow your car in the way I did. The fact is my wife had gone into labour and my own car broke down on the way to the hospital not far from your house. This was a real emergency and I needed a car on the quick and I had no time to knock and ask your help. She gave birth to our little girl within minutes of our getting there, so that shows how close things were.

'Now things have settled down again, I am returning your car with our thanks. I am also enclosing a couple of tickets for the Palladium, which I'd bought for the missus and me but which of course we can't now go because of the baby. So I hope you and your wife will accept them with our thanks. Please enjoy the show, and again I can only apologise for any inconvenience I have caused you.'

Naturally the note had been unsigned, though from the scribbled handwriting and the amount of space the writer had spent apologising, it hadn't been hard to guess who the tealeaf that nicked the car was. The tickets of course, had been kosher.

I took the note out of my jacket and passed it over to my one-time partner. He took it and made a very dramatic show of peering closely at it, occasionally gave me a furtive look as he read it. Then he put it back on the table in front of me, and looked up in what was supposed to be astonishment.

'Blimey, Nicker. You never fell for this old gag did ya? I mean, we've pulled stunts like this in the old days ourselves', he breathed, going all Marlon Brando on me.

I smiled at the memory of our partnership, which had been years before I'd linked up with MoMo (Maurice Morris). It hadn't lasted long – in fact it had come to an end after Willie had been put away for the umpteenth time for some ridiculous job he'd gone private on.

In fact, apart from MoMo and people like Armlock Harry Foster, few people actually knew that Willie and I had ever even worked together. Well, it wasn't the wisest thing to brag about in our community. and I had insisted on it staying that way. Mr Martin you see, has always been one of life's great losers. I had always been the planner, while Willie (and now MoMo) had been the crew, neither of them particularly blessed with the greatest number of brain cells.

He'd never been nicked working on a job with me, and he'd never found it necessary or particularly advisable to shop me either. He was a runt, but Will was no grass and in any case would have known better. He knew that if I ever went down thanks to him, he would pay a much heftier price than the odd bit of porridge for dipping pockets. I jerked myself back to reality, gave him a rueful grin and shrugged.

'Yes, mate. I know; but I fell for it. Me and Liz went to see Ken Dodd last night with the tickets. Good show actually.'

'And?' He didn't want to ask, but felt he had to.

'Well, what do you think? Doddie's shows always overrun anyway and while we was in the West End, the git who sent the tickets done our place over. I must be mad falling for that old scam, but I did.'

'Oh Gawd', he seemed to be afraid to carry the conversation on, but knew he had to. 'Did they get much?'

'Only one thing. What they were looking for all the time, I guess. Remember the diamond necklace I bought Liz out of the Granby job five years ago?'

Between ourselves, it was worth ten grand but I'd only paid a couple of thousand quid for it, because it was still a bit 'warm' when I bought it. Now it was a lot cooler, and in no danger of starring on Crime Watch, it was worth a lot more dosh. The news of it being nicked seemed to shake Willie up a bit, as though he hadn't expected that.

I glanced over at him. He'd clearly had quite a shock, and was spluttering over the whisky at my words – hardly the reaction one would have expected from 'an old buddy' to the bad news that I had been robbed.

'Good Gawd', he said, once again calling on the Almighty to cover his confusion. 'Was it insured?'

As it happens it was – but I'd had to wait a few years until it had cooled down a bit before phoning the Norwich Union.

'Of course it was. That's why I'm not too bothered. It was worth about ten grand to the insurance company, which is probably why McIver has a scene of crime officer in my house as we speak', I lied. I knew the reference to Chief Inspector McIver would make him even more uncomfortable. He swallowed down the last of the whisky as he rose to his feet.

'Sorry to hear about all that, Nicker, but at least you'll still have the insurance money, won't ya? he muttered before almost rushing out of the pub.

I watched him disappear into the street before putting on my gloves and carefully picking up the note he'd very carelessly left his prints all over. Carefully I folded it back into its original form before tucking it into my inside pocket. My dabs were on it anyway of course but clearly I would have read it anyway, so they were bound to have been on it. Willies were on there too, and fresher, but it's as well to make sure. Then, using my nice clean handkerchief to pick up his glass, I wrapped it up in it very carefully before putting it into my jacket pocket. There it nestled happily against the necklace, which had accompanied Liz and me to the Palladium the night before.

That shows just what a right little plonker Willie is. He sends you posh tickets for a West End show that your missus is almost certain to wear her best tomfoolery at. Then he breaks in to try and nick her best necklace while we were out. He'd probably forgotten we'd pulled the same stroke ourselves years ago.

He'd been right in one thing though – the insurance would come in very handy and once I've got a mate in Amsterdam to redesign it, Liz can wear it to a police concert if she wants – not that we ever get invited to one of them.

First I had to nip home with a whisky glass full of fingerprints, and an apologetic note equally revealing before calling the filth and reporting a burglary. Oh yeah, McIver and his forensic fools are going to love this one.

It had been a good show, as well!

23

Dagenham Posted

Have they closed the tripe mines?

During the war, as Uncle Albert Trotter used to say, for obvious reasons food was a bit of a problem for mothers in particular. Our mum grew it, queued for it, or sent us to the allotments in Chadwell Heath to nick carrots and cabbages while the owner was at work. We munched through sawdust sausages, chewed rubbery dried egg, and downed platefuls of stew with pieces of scrag-end floating defiantly among the dumplings and stolen carrots. God, how I hated mutton!

In fact, not everything was rationed. Offal may have only been available at the whim of the butcher, but you needed no points or coupons if you caught him in a good mood. That was probably why I developed a passion for tripe and onions.

Even today my taste buds still tingle with excitement at the memory of those gristly tenderised pieces of cow-stomach, cooked in milk and onions to share a soup-plate with good honest boiled spuds. After we married Dearly Beloved got my mother's tripe and onions recipe and, though she never actually tasted it herself, did a pretty good version of it for me. Then, suddenly, it all stopped. Along with stewed eels and pig's trotters, tripe and onions became part of a nostalgia trip.

I have to admit it would have been an acquired taste, based on that good old fashioned family 'take it or leave it' menu, with the added verbal blackmail that lots of starving children in Europe would have loved to be able to eat it. I mean, she was probably right as far as that was concerned but Ivy Lynch was quite unscrupulous when it came to persuading her kids to eat their greens. She had some pretty good emotional lines about tripe as well.

Knowing what our reaction would probably have been if we knew the truth she told us that it came out of the Welsh tripe mines, where brave men were risking their lives to get it. This of course kept us ignorant of the true source of our dinner, and even made us feel patriotic about eating it.

This was the same woman who, when food convoys carrying only essential foods were being sunk in the Atlantic, unashamedly convinced us that the mashed swede flavoured with banana essence she put on our bread for tea, was real banana spread. She also persuaded us that a pan fried mixture of mashed potatoes and the hated greens i.e. bubble and squeak, was what Spitfire pilots had for lunch every day because it was good for their eyes. I tell you when it came to conning her kids, that woman could have lied for England, bless her, though even she could not persuade us to try the sheep's heard out father was so fond of, and I was never keen on things like corned beef rissoles either.

I know things have changed. We had a fishmonger in Valence Circus (next to the 'Continental Butcher' who sold horse meat) who would invite us to pick out one of the eels squirming around in a shallow metal tank on his marble slabs. We'd watch in awe as he decapitated the poor little sod we'd chosen, gutted it, chopped it up into chunks, and wrapped it up with some parsley in greaseproof paper for us to take home.

Stewed eels is another of those dishes I can only savour in memory these days, though the jellied version is still there to remind us of what life was when Cook's eel and pie shop (with its green liquor), reigned alongside the chippie as our fast food outlet. Nowadays you can get a frozen version in Sainsburys which is a passable substitute, but there was a certain atmosphere and smell about the old eel and pie shop which you don't get at home.

Still In My Own Lynchtime

I suppose one positive is that they don't sell much mutton any more either, but where's the tripe? Presumably cows do still have stomachs – several – and we do still see them munching our meadows. Pigs still do have feet, don't they? I know they do because I've seen them on telly.

Its been years since I stopped believing my mother's porkies about the tripe mines of course, but it does appear to have vanished from our lives, other than in the tins we feed Jack, our spaniel, with. Come to think of it, he doesn't even seem to like it.

Is there, perhaps, another EU regulation forbidding the sale of tripe? If so then perhaps a new sort of booze cruise, – a 'tripe trip' – across the Channel where they don't seem to take much notice of EU regulations anyway, might be in order.

After all, why should Jack get all the pleasure?

24

Dagenham Posted

Whacko

Those of a particular age will remember comedian Jimmy Edwards' TV show Whacko, in which he was a headmaster whose sole method of handling miscreant boys was with the persuasive powers of 'the cane'. If he tried it now he'd have solicitors crawling all over him, and social workers trying to justify their existence by saying child violence was nothing to joke about.

Well, it never was – but that never stopped us being 'slippered', 'palm ruler'd' or getting the odd clump round the ears. We also needed to dodge flying blackboard rubbers and lumps of chalk, just for appearing to be daydreaming. I was once even put on trial in class by a physics master who accused me, accurately as it happens, of pushing past him onto a bus in the evening, resulting in his being left at the bus stop. He got a result.

I think the memory that sank in most of all though was that of the school's head, Mr Claude Arthur, going into public whacking mode over some books. The South East Tech was divided into two – the main school in Longbridge Road (now a University) and the junior school in Rosslyn Road, Barking, presided over by Mrs Coleman with Claude being the ultimate hot shot.

Lunchtimes, once we'd got past the grief of school dinners, most of us spent kicking a ball around in the playground, or just hanging around in groups. We were doing that one day when some of the kids started offering us cheap Ian Allen train and bus spotters books. They were giveaway prices but I turned them down.

Not for reasons of honesty and integrity (being a Scout) you understand, so much as I was permanently skint, and couldn't even afford even their rock bottom prices. It went on for a week or two before the authorities, in the shape of a couple of coppers, struck. It appears that the books were on offer because they were the result of a team of organised shoplifters from 2B who'd been nicking them from Wilson and Whitworths opposite Barking Station.

Caught bang to rights, they not only confessed but also even grassed on the kids who had bought their ill-gotten gains. Somehow the school calmed W and W down, presumably refunding the dosh, and assured them things would be sorted. Gawd – how they were sorted! I think it was the only time in my life when poverty actually paid off.

We were all questioned, with the buyers getting detentions and having to pay the full cost. Then the entire junior school was ordered to report to 'the hall' in Longbridge Road one afternoon and, not being entirely sure why, we straggled the couple of miles to the main school. There we were all sat down along with the rest of the senior school as well, to wait.

The teachers – many of them in full kit with mortarboards and gowns – filed onto the platform. Then six of our schoolmates – instantly recognisable as the tealeaves who'd been flogging the books, also filed onto the platform. We began to experience the same feelings of awe the mobs waiting for the guillotine victims to suffer, would have felt. Not excitement because this was very clearly a very serious occasion.

Finally Claude himself strode onto the stage to talk to us. He began to harangue us about some kids bringing disgrace upon our school by nicking things from local shops. He told us that each of the kids on stage was about to receive retribution. Then, as the others watched in mounting fear, he began with the nearest trembling backside to him.

That man pulled no punches that day. He wielded the cane

he produced with such vicious venom we all winced at every thud – the recipients screeched out loud. It must have been even more agonising for those kids still waiting to be whacked as he made his way down the line towards through them, especially the last one. We had been urged from an early age to show that we could stand pain, but believe me there was no stiff upper lip with those lads that day.

To be honest, I don't think any of us in that hall ever transgressed again either.

25

Dagenham Posted

Anyone can make a mistake!

I did something in July that I haven't done for years – I 'hopped the wag' from Stevens Road school and since this was the second time I've done it I am hoping the result will not be as painful for me as it was last time. Then it was Ginger Barrett's fault and happened at a time we were ducking German raiders – this time it was down to a hot day and a German radiator.

I'd pledged to go to the school to talk to some of the kids about what a different place it is now, than what schools were like in my day. Actually I was quite looking forward to it, and I left Brentwood in good time on a hot and sunny day.

Sixty-plus years ago I also left home in good time – and it was only about half a mile away down the Avenue, but it was also already a warm and sunny day. Ginger lived a couple of doors away and we had our 'bushes' – the strip of land dividing the dual carriageway which was then full of shrubs, trees and bushes – to wander through.

Well, by the time we actually reached the gates of Stevens Road – usually packed with a throng of grizzling kids and mums desperate to unload them onto the school– it was empty. Not a tearful child or anxious mother in sight – in fact there was no sign of life. Ginger summed up the situation straight away.

'They must be closed for the day', he said joyfully, and I was only too glad to agree. Obviously we'd missed the announcement the previous day that there would be no school, and there was nothing for it but to go home again – through the bushes of course.

There was no point in actually going into HQ to report once we'd reached our part of the Avenue. So, once Ginger and I had got bored bouncing off the bushes and crawling through the undergrowth, we marked out a hopscotch pitch on the paving stones outside his house and started playing there.

Now my father was a London busman (throughout the blitz as it happens) and often had to work what was called a spreadover shift, which meant a few hours in the morning followed by a few hours break and then a few more hours in the late afternoon or evening. During those periods between the shifts he'd come home for a spot of lunch, a quick kip or to dig over his vegetable patch.

This time when he popped home, it was to see his eldest playing hopscotch with his mate in the street, instead of slaving over a hot slab of plasticine. He was, to put it mildly, a bit curious.

'Why aren't you at school?' he demanded in a fairly threatening voice.

I explained that Ginger and I had turned up at the school to find it closed so we'd come home again, but he didn't seem to believe me. In fact he grabbed me by the scruff of the neck and propelled me rather rapidly back in the direction of Stevens Road.

When we got there I pointed to the still empty gates and said 'See?' but he never seemed to be taking notice as he dragged me up the driveway, past the piles of boiler coke, and into the school itself. There, I was amazed to see, the classrooms seemed to be full, and clearly the headmistress was not prepared to back up my story about the school being closed.

I was ushered into my classroom and there, in front of a chorus of sniggering and giggling, I was ordered to spend the rest of the morning in a corner reflecting over my misdemeanour. Dad went home and clearly told my mother all about it because

Still In My Own Lynchtime

when I did get home for lunch, I was given a b.... good hiding by her as well.

The lesson sunk in because I never truanted again – well, until July when, on one of the hottest days of the century, my German motor decided that to have a good old boil up on the A12 on the way to Stevens Road, might be a good idea. By the time the RAC arrived to bail me out, it was too late to continue to school anyway.

Never even had Ginger to blame this time either.

26

Dagenham Posted

'ancock, Robin, and Cap'n Jim

A couple of years after my sea-going phase was over I found myself in an old Barking church pledging all my worldly goods to one Elizabeth Rose Denyer – at least that was the name she arrived at the church with. She walked out of there as Liz Lynch of course to start what has been over forty-two (so far) years of married strife... sorry, life!

We'd met in a Manor Park glue factory – well at least Wilme Collier did used to make wallpaper – which had been foresighted enough to offer me some employment as an assistant maintenance engineer. Our eyes met across a crowded conveyor belt and the rest is family history. We courted in the pubs and cinemas of Ilford, Dagenham, Barking and Leicester Square, dined out in the new 'Chicken Inns', and canoodled in darkened shop doorways or at her front gate.

All fairly predictable, but apart from her breaking with tradition to propose to me, I guess the final outcome was down to three men in particular – Anthony Aloysius 'ancock, Robin Hood and Captain James Cook.

Thinking about those three, one killed himself, another bled to death in a wood and the third got savaged on a beach. Topped, flopped and chopped, but now I have your interest draw up a barrel, he hearties and I'll tell all.

Still In My Own Lynchtime

Back in the late fifties/early sixties there was only one television programme that could be described as compulsive viewing – Hancock's Half Hour. It went out on black and white screens at 8pm on Friday nights, and was the first television show to empty the streets. In fact so many people stayed at home to watch Hancock instead of going out for a Friday evening pint or three, some pubs even began to install a television set over the bar.

The Robin Hood in Longbridge Road was one, and since Dearly Beloved then lived in Barking and me in Becontree Avenue, it was a very handy place to pop into for a quick Red Barrel (me) and Port and Lemon (her) at the right time to catch the show. We did that one night, found a table close to the bar and with a good view of the telly, and settled down in a packed pub to watch Hancock and Sid James while quaffing a glass or two of ale (Babycham in her case).

It was a great show that night, and it wasn't long before the entire pub was roaring loudly at the antics of our heroes. Suddenly I noticed DB saying something but it was during a burst of laughter so didn't hear her. I cupped my ear to show that and this time she shouted her question.

Now there come moments in all television comedy shows when the laughter subsides, to give the jokers a chance to crack new gags etc. It was at precisely such a moment that my companion raised her voice to go above the hubbub – except there suddenly wasn't noise, and the entire pub heard her.

'Have you got any intention of marrying me?' she blurted out at full volume, before realising Hancock had been forgotten in the pub and we were suddenly the centres of attention of tables and chairs all around us.

Now, you have to remember that in those days a question phrased like that had certain implications. They usually involved irate parents or, in my case, another hurried look at my seaman's discharge book to see if going back to sea might be an option. Not that I had much time to think, because I was choking and coughing on a mouthful of Watney's and spraying the stuff in all directions.

Right across the saloon bar of the Robin heads were turned

away from Hancock for a few embarrassing seconds, to home in on a crimson-faced young girl and her spluttering beau. Fortunately Hancock proved the greater draw and it wasn't long before we were left to ourselves again. Once I'd recovered from the shock of her question, and wiped my face and chin clear of Red Barrel, I hurriedly reassured her that I had every intention of doing so, but that I had been waiting for my own moment to bring the topic up. Oh yes, and before you ask, she wasn't!

She lived in Barking so her parish church St Margaret's was a natural choice anyway, but then I discovered that a personal seafaring hero, Captain Cook, had plighted his troth there. Well, what was good enough for Capn Jim was certainly good enough for former 4th Engineer Lynch, so on August 25th (Liberation Day in France as it happens) 1962 we did the biz there too.

Now, over four decades and four kids later, Hancocks gone, Cooks history and even the Robin Hood is now a Longbridge Road building site, but Liz – I really did have every intention of proposing, honest!

27

VIEWPOINT

Gun law

There was a time, and it doesn't seem that long ago when criminals going out on a blagging (robbery with violence) searched each other to make sure none of them was 'tooled up' (carrying a gun). It wasn't with any thought of pity for their victims, as much as to protect their own necks.

Then our leaders abolished the death penalty, and now we have gun law on our streets. Young thugs used to carry razors and coshes, now they carry automatic and semi-automatic weapons or vicious killing knives.

They used to fight, and slash each other with blades, in milk bars – now they gun each other down in burger bars and in the streets. They even stab each other in schools, with no thought of the outcome.

There are, and remain, many good reasons for abolishing the death penalty, with the obvious fact that mistakes can be made and innocent men hung, being a foremost one. In recent years we have seen many instances of innocent men (and women) being freed after spending years in jail before their names were cleared.

But the fact is that now we live in a far more violent society than we did even during the era of the Krays and Richardsons, whose violence was usually directed at people in their own line of work We live in one where women of 90-plus are beaten up, raped and even killed and where innocent bystanders or passers by can get cut down as a result of gang wars.

We hear criminals, and their lawyers, bleating about their human rights, with politicians and the judiciary appearing to be only too anxious to listen. But what about the human rights of ordinary law abiding people, who just want to be able to walk the streets without fear.

Why do we have to suffer this lawless society? Because, from the early days, the punishment doesn't fit the crime. Lose discipline in the schools, and you encourage criminality. Even schoolyard misdemeanours are glossed over because the kids 'know their rights', and because teachers live in fear of legal sanctions and a compensation culture, which grows rich because corporal punishment is no longer an option.

Yes it is easy to laugh at, and dismiss, the 'hanging and flogging' brigade as being a throwback to earlier days. But in those earlier days fewer people were gunned down or knifed to death on the streets, let alone in their own homes.

The cane was not a terminal punishment, albeit a painful one, and the gallows could always be averted by reprieve. So let head's punish with the short sharp shock treatment that may just discourage a future gunman. Let those prospective gun murderers always have the fear of the condemned cell in their minds even if they are sure a reprieve will save their life. Sure is not certain, and the point is that while the killer can be reprieved, the killed cannot.

Those who carry a gun, or a knife, cannot by any stretch of the imagination plead innocence. They carry them to threaten and ultimately to kill, and do so in the full knowledge that at the very worst they will only get prison. The old habits about gang members searching each other before going on a job, no longer apply.

I recognise that no Home Secretary wants to agonise over whether or not to reprieve a murderer, but if such a gesture was almost automatic, leaving just the faint possibility that it may not be granted, it might concentrate some minds wonderfully. It could save lives!

28

Dagenham Posted

Pope Jim

As you get older, you tend to start taking religion a little more seriously than perhaps you would have done even ten years earlier. I don't believe that is necessarily a reflection on the beliefs that have sustained you over the years, be they agnostic, atheist or whatever. It is more a case of age starting to make you focus a little harder on what happens next... just in case.

In a manner of speaking, I guess I had what should have been a fairly religious background myself – the firstborn of a Protestant mother and a Roman Catholic 'Pope'. Well, Dad wasn't a real Pope of course, but by all accounts in those days they would do anything for a pair of shoes, as I will explain.

We were brought up in a very different world, as far as faith goes, compared with today's. Wartime, with the Luftwallies aiming bombs at them, did tend to concentrate people's minds a bit, and in those times all the churches were well attended. A few hundred yards from our house in Becontree Avenue we had a Methodist and Anglican churches, a Chapel of a denomination I cannot recall, and a Catholic church. We had a synagogue just up the road near our school, and Salvation Army midwives living next door.

There were moments, years after the blitz during the latter part of the war, when we prayed quite a lot. That was when the unmistakeable noise of the engine of a 'doodlebug' rasping merrily on it's way above us, suddenly stopped rasping merrily on it's way. That could only mean one thing. It was the moment a thousand prayers within earshot, were hurriedly muttered – begging for the bloody thing to fall on someone else's street, or even better on our school.

As children we were always encouraged, well ordered, to say our routine bedtime prayers. Night after night we went through the 'God Bless Mummy and Daddy' bit, being sure to include all the grannies, granddad, aunts and uncles, and with a special mention for 'Uncle John who is a prisoner of war'. Mum supervised just to make sure we were tucked into bed as devout little Christians. Not that she was much in the way of devout herself.

For some reason or other she also insisted, once we reached the appropriate age, that we attended the Sunday School in the Methodist church around the corner. I don't think it was because she particularly coveted the religious texts we brought home, or even the fundraising lavender 'scent cards' that came home just as regularly. I think it was the attraction of having an hour or so of peace and quiet on a Sunday afternoon.

Sunday School never turned me against religion – but then, it never turned me onto it either. In fairness I suppose it gave us a kind of morality standard, although Mum carried a pretty useful right-hand clump to discourage any criminal instincts as well.

Being brought up in a household where one of the parents is a Catholic and the other is not, sometimes does cause complications – especially as far as the Catholics are concerned, or at least were in those days. Even today many of them see it still as a 'mixed marriage' of the sort they do not welcome or even, in some extreme cases, recognise.

Between the wars, when Jimmy Lynch from Wapping was courting Ivy Lacey from East Ham, the divisions were even more acute. As I understand it, the news that Dad was courting a Protestant woman would have been about as popular as Margaret Thatcher was with the Young Socialists in the seventies. Apparently this was even more so with his local priest who, it seems, was appalled at the very idea and decided to rush to the rescue.

Now to be honest Dad never had much time for any church. Born in 1908, he had grown up in real grinding East End poverty, and had never understood why the church encouraged big families. He never agreed with its disapproval of any kind of birth control other than less effective natural ones.

'Son, do not talk to me of the 'good old days' because they were nothing of the sort. We had nothing to eat, and no shoes on our feet. When we went to church every Sunday the blokes often had bottles of beer stuck in their skies (sky rockets – pockets), and couldn't wait for the service to finish so they could get back to the pub again – yet we never had two ha'pennies to rub together. They spent all the money they did get on booze,' he often remarked, with a great deal of bitterness, pointing out that many of the women had been just as bad when it came to drink.

So he grew up with a lot of disdain for religion in general and the Catholic church he had been brought up in and educated by, in particular. (Get him on the subject of nuns teaching and he was an education in itself) He was a very strong Labour Party and Trade Union man, and his socialism meant more to him than any kind of religion.

So clearly, his view of the church didn't ease much when his local priest, reacted badly to the awful news that Dad was not only about to marry a Protestant, but going to do so in a non-Catholic church. He hotfooted it round to the house to talk him out of it.

I only have family legend and what Dad told me to go on, but I wish I had been there. The priest got off to a bad start apparently by referring to Dad's fiancé, my future mum, as 'this woman'. He then went further over the top by implying that any children resulting from this proposed 'unholy union' would not be legitimate. Now, in those days illegitimacy was a real stigma for any child to carry, even though it wasn't the kid's fault. By all accounts the old man went bananas at the suggestion that his kids would be little bastards.

I understand several of his brothers, my uncles, had to hold him down, while the priest made his escape with Dad shouting a few home truths at him as he fled. It must have marked the final breakdown in Dad's relationship with the Vatican – a relationship that had once even one elected him Pope. Well, sort of, and it was only to get a pair of boots!

It happened in the annual Catholic 'procession' when he was a kid. (An event which, strangely enough given his views, he always insisted we went to Stepney as, a family to watch, in the years immediately after the war). It seems that in his day the local kids who took part were given a pair of shoes, which to urchins raking the East End streets barefoot in the early years of the 20th century, must have seemed an attractive offer. I always had difficulty actually believing that claim of his, until I saw photos of kids in rags (who may well have included him) taken during that period.

Anyway, it seems that one year Dad was picked for the starring role – Pope for the day. One can just imagine the pride and joy felt by his deeply Catholic Irish mother Bridget (Granny Lynch to us) as she watched her son pass by in all his pomp and glory as Pope Jim. It was years before Dad admitted this to me. As a young mother, despite her religion, 'Biddy Lynch' had been quite a local firebrand – not above brawling in the street with neighbours while the worse for drink.

She was something else, to be honest. A few years before she died, after having been knocked down by a motorcyclist in Burdett Road, some guy had tried to mug her, only to get beaten up himself as she used her umbrella on him until he fled. Nevertheless she was always allegedly very religious, as most of them were in those days.

As far the beliefs of this son of 'Pope Jim' are concerned, I have always kept an open mind. There were many occasions when this, er self proclaimed Protestant, has also been a Catholic or Jew. Church parades in the Royal Navy always began with an inspection followed by a religious service. Before the service began the Master at Arms bellowed out 'Catholics and Jews – fall out!' whereupon, a growing number each week, broke ranks and doubled off parade very smartly. This was no sudden 'road to Damascus' – it meant we could get to the NAAFI bar before the

Still In My Own Lynchtime

CofE lot did, and no one ever questioned our faith conversion because they were all at church parade.

I have found 'God' in some strange places though. I remember when I was in the Fort Avalon, trading up and down the American and Canadian East Coast, we got caught out in quite a violent North Atlantic storm. We came out of it ok, but a German training ship (sails and masts etc) in the same area, went down and was lost with all hands, most of them young boys.

For some reason our skipper, Captain Baxter-Powell, decided to hold a church service at sea as a sort of tribute to the boys who had lost their lives with the ship. As a ship's officer I had to attend anyway, but what surprised me a little was the reaction of the crew. This was just over ten years after the war, don't forget – and they were quite emotional. It was the first time I ever really experienced the 'comradeship of the sea' tradition, and it was quite moving especially when you remember that some of those men may well have faced hazard from German U-boats a decade or so earlier.

I cannot claim to be a churchgoer in the 'regular' sort of sense although I do claim to live by a moral code formed by Sunday School biblical basics and childhood good hidings. I also, and this would probably surprise my kids, pop into a church occasionally – just to sit there on my own and reflect on things in general. I suppose, however, my oddest religious experience brings me full circle back to 'Pope Jim' again.

A year or so after Mum died in Oldchurch hospital, Dad suddenly collapsed and was taken to the same hospital. Unbeknown to us he had been having problems he hadn't mentioned to us – his kidneys had collapsed and stopped working. He was talking gibberish when they took him in because, apparently, the loss of the use of your kidneys tends to poison the brain.

They got them going again and his mind cleared as they did so – but the really bad news was the cancerous growth they found on the kidneys. I was told he would never leave the hospital alive. His mind was also flitting in and out of lucidity – he would be rational one moment, and totally out of it the next.

He hung on there for a month, and it was a grim time for all of us of course, but all his family and friends, visited him every day and evening. Dad, in his more lucid moments, kept talking about coming home, but we all knew the truth though we had kept it from him.

One night I was visiting him on my own. The conversation had begun well, but he had drifted off more and more into his own mysterious and private world of gibberish and irrationality. But just before I was about to leave I saw a priest coming through the ward on his visits and I waylaid him.

Briefly I gave him Dad's history as a lapsed Catholic, and how apart from weddings and funerals he had not been near a church of any sort in over fifty years, and certainly not made any confession. I wondered if there was a last service I could do for him. *'He is very very ill and he won't understand you,'* I told the priest, who responded very positively, when I asked him to give Dad some kind of last rites.

Dad was still conscious, but muttering incoherently, as the priest drew the curtains around the bed and made his preparations. I stood next to him as he went into his last rites routine, telling Dad about the long journey he was about to embark on, with glory etc at the end of it.

I then witnessed the most astonishing religious moment of my life. Dad, on his back and propped up by his pillows, began to respond to the priest's words, although he could still not get his own ones out properly. It was as if something had managed to break through into that poor befuddled mind. There is no doubt in my mind that he was actually trying to make the right responses. I was astounded – but more was to come.

The priest finished, and we pulled the curtains back from around the bed again. I shook hands with the priest, and thanked him for what he'd done. Somehow I felt a little better in myself that, despite all his feelings about religion, I had been able with that simple act, to put Dad back in touch with his roots again – even if he didn't know about it.

I turned to him, waved goodbye and casually said. *'I'll see you tomorrow, Dad'*, not expecting much of a reply.

At that moment – as clear and as lucid as ever I heard him

speak – he spoke, gesturing towards the departing priest and with a grin on his face.

'Right – but don't you bring him with you next time!'

I laughed, and left. I never saw him alive again, because he died that night before I could get back to the hospital.

He was a great man, our Dad. A product of the slums, who fought his way out of the East End, through sheer guts and determination, hard work and the love of his wife, our mother. Their roots left both of them determined that their own children, myself, Roy and Patricia, should not have to suffer as they had.

Best of all, he left me laughing. God bless you, Pope Jim!

29

American hospitality

Although I have not been there in nearly fifty years, when those hijacked 'flying bombs' ripped the heart out of Manhattan a few years back, they took a little bit of me too. I just loved that city.

I'd arrived there under a bit of a cloud in the mid fifties (see chapter 6) because, having crossed the Atlantic in the French liner Ile de France largely in the drinking company of a Russian diplomat, the FBI appeared to be very reluctant to let me in. In fact it viewed me with a great deal of suspicion suspicion, questioning me very aggressively when we docked.

New York was a revelation to a young man straight off the bombsites of London – all day TV (rubbish but it was all day), shops open till the early hours of the morning, burger stands selling wonderfully cold pineapple juice on every corner, and gun-shops not selling just rifles and pistols but even with light artillery pieces standing outside on the pavement like we put A-boards outside our shops in Dagenham today.

The World Trade Centre didn't exist then of course, but I did the Empire State, joined the 'sidewalk supervisors' watching pizza cooks doing their stuff in the windows of the pizza parlours, wandered over to the UN and had a steak in Jack Dempsey's restaurant. I also overdid it on the local booze one night and, failing miserably in my attempts to find a public toilet, had a bit of an embarrassing accident on Broadway – now forever in my mind the Great Wet Way.

It was very different from 1957 London, which even then still had its share of bombsites – most of them by then second-hand car sales pitches – anti-social drinking hours and skint Londoners. New York was big, brash, bold, and I loved it.

The SS Fort Avalon sailed in and out of the Big Apple almost every month, usually docking in Bush Terminal in Brooklyn where 'da guys' spoke Brooklynese, a kind of Cockney American that in a way made me feel more at home than in the ship where I was surrounded by Scots, Geordies, Scousers and Newfies (Newfoundlanders).

I don't care what they say about New Yorkers, I found them open hearted and generous. Their dockies were always happy to pay the best prices for any duty free liquor that happened to find its way past the dockside revenue (customs) officers, and even invited us into their homes. Well at least Joe did.

Joe (I never did learn his second name) was the foreman of the gang of marine fitters who came aboard when we docked in Brooklyn, to fill the maintenance contract that kept the ship on top line.

At sea we were expected to keep the Fort Avalon doing it's 'Dirty British Coaster' bit, chugging up and down from New York to Maine (New Brunswick), Halifax in Nova Scotia, St Johns and Cornerbrook in Newfoundland and (sometimes) down to Bermuda.

New York was our home port though and was where Joe and his lads did all the major engine-room repairs and boiler cleaning jobs. Nice guys – always ready to join us in Otto's Bar just down the street outside Bush Terminal for a bottle or three of Ballantyne's or Budweiser beer.

So it was that, one day when it was getting close to Christmas, the Second, Third, Fourth Engineers and myself (I was Fifth Engineer by then) had been drinking ourselves into a touch of the homesick hump. Much as we enjoyed the social life of the Avalon, and the British Merchant Navy Officers Club in Manhattan, they were not home. Joe came up from the engine room to talk to Bill Thomas, our Second Engineer, and was soon doing his best to empty our case of beer and picking up our moodys at the same time.

"Hell, why doncha come and stay with us for the weekend?"

he invited, clearly meaning every word he slurred. Well, whether he did or not, we took him up on it anyway and he agreed to pick us up on the Saturday morning.

So by mid-morning on Saturday we were driving out of New York City into what was clearly countryside (you could tell by the cows and horses). We drove for about an hour before Joe says, 'Here we are, guys', and swung the car into a drive that looked like the M25 on a quiet day, at the end of which there stood an even more impressive huge house.

Maisie, Joe's wife, fussed over us from the moment we arrived, making sure we lacked for nothing. The four of us were each allocated a bedroom, so you can imagine how big this place was – and Joe was only the foreman of a work gang. The guy was either very shrewd on the stock exchange, or he was on the take somewhere.

We had a brilliant day and even more so in the evening when a load of Joe and Maisie's friends and family turned up. It turned into a real party with no lack of food or drink, and with the four Limeys just loving being the centre of attention.

Now, within minutes of our arrival in her home Maisie had introduced us to her icebox – the biggest refrigerator we'd ever seen. Even better, it was full – beers, Cokes, all kinds of meats and groceries and a huge plate of cooked chicken legs – well chicken quarters really, but the plate was piled high with them.

"Hey guys – this is open house, and if you get hungry at all while you're here, just come and help yourself to whatever you want. Cold chicken, sandwich, beer, whatever," she told us.

Well, late that night when everyone was asleep I took her up on her offer. I had lain awake and suddenly a beer and sandwich sounded rather attractive. I crept downstairs and helped myself, just as Maisie had said we could. Then I had a thought – well it was such a big plate of chicken pieces. I nicked four, wrapped them up in napkins and tucked them into the pocket of my big overcoat.

We all, even the English atheists, went to church the next morning – and then after Sunday lunch and a lot more booze, we had to say our farewells, and Joe drove us back to Bush Terminal.

Still In My Own Lynchtime

It really had been a great weekend, and I will always remember with gratitude that wonderful couple and their hospitality.

Back on board we did what we always did – one got some booze in his cabin and the rest of us went along to help him get shot of it. After a few cans had seen the light of the waste-bin, I announced that I had a present for them. I pulled the napkins from my coat and cheerfully announced that I had captured some chicken for supper.

There was a stunned silence, and for a moment I thought I had broken a code or something – but after all, Maisie had told us to help ourselves. Then, wordlessly, Second Engineer, the Third and then the Fourth got up, went to their cabins and came back with napkins full of chicken bits and put them onto the table.

Oh yeah, we knew how to abuse hospitality on the Avalon.

30

Dagenham Posted

Hitler tried to kill me

Having written about my schoolboy pals in the 'Mild Bunch' – the two Leslies (Blythe and Barratt) – the power of the Dagenham Post was such that within days I was reunited with them – well, verbally by phone.

It was really great to talk to them for the first time in over half a century since the government broke us up with its insistence that we learn how to kill Russians for a couple of years. Then I went off to sea and we never really got back in touch, even when I came ashore for good.

There will always be a special bond between us though – we played football and cricket together, scrumped apples together, and we nearly got killed together, when only my father's cack-handedness saved our lives. So, now I have your attention switch off your mobile phones and settle down while I tell you how Dad foiled Hitler's last desperate pop at the Mild Bunch. I can even pinpoint the date – February 3rd, 1945, a matter of weeks before he blew his brains out. Serves him right too!

We never had the kind of patent leather football they play with now. Ours was a heavy leather panelled job with a painful lace (if you headed it in the wrong place) and footbreakingly soggy in the rain and mud. More relevantly it had an inflatable 'bladder' inside.

Still In My Own Lynchtime

In February 1945 the ball that 'Buddy', 'Ginger' and I, played with happened to be mine, but sadly it needed pumping up. Dad offered to do it in time for us to take it over Goodmayes Park the following day, but there was always a problem when it came to pumping these balls up. Once the bladder had been fully inflated inside the rubber tube connected to it, into which the pump was inserted, needed to be shoved back into the ball before it was laced up again.

Once the puncture had been mended and the pump put to good use, Dad used the end of a tablespoon to press it all into place. 'Bang!' – it slipped and went right through the rubber bladder. This time it was to badly damaged to be repaired and, even if we had the time and money (which we didn't), there was no time to get a new bladder.

The next day I had to break the news to the lads, and we decided to go over the park anyway and watch a match. This game was at the other end of the park to the field we usually played on, and would have been playing on if we'd had a ball. We watched it anyway and suddenly, midway through the first half, a plume of smoke suddenly arched across the horizon in front of us and plunged into the other side of the park. It was a V2, and it made a helluva bang and a massive hole exactly where our coats would have been goalposts.

Everyone hit the deck of course, because that is what we instinctively did anyway, but after a few minutes the game restarted and we watched it until the ref blew his whistle. In retrospect this might seem a bit casual now, but we'd spent five years getting used to bangs and bombs, and we knew our priorities. Once the match was over we strolled over to the other side of the park to see the crater (which later became a boating lake).

There had been a casualty, but not in the park. A bloke in the barber's across the road had been 'trusting his hair to Sydney's care' (according to Sydney's slogan on his wall) when the blast damaged his window – though not so much as he'd damaged the guys neck with the open razor he'd been shaving him with.

My mother was in Sainsburys in Green Lanes a few hundred yards away (in those days that shop was all marble counters and queues) when she'd heard that a rocket had fallen on Goodmayes Park. She dropped everything and rushed home to tell Dad, and send him up the park.

This would have been over an hour after the rocket had fallen, and my lack of presence by then filled them both with dread. Also alarmed, the old man hotfooted it to the park to check it out, and arrived only to find us strolling casually away from it after rubbernecking the crater.

They were so pleased to get me home in one piece, I got a bloody good hiding for not reporting in straight away. So Hitler did get a bit of a result in one way!

31

SOAPBOX

If it's good enough for the Yanks…

Once again the rumour factory is hard at work, with the spinners whipping up the idea of cancelling some local government elections pending possible abolition of some councils. This government has long abandoned the old concept of, *'if it works, don't fix it'* to replace it with *'if it doesn't work for us, fix it'* and appears to be determined to push on with its already rejected dreams of regional assemblies.

It's only a few years since the last town hall 'reorganisation' when, among other things, councillors were allowed to vote themselves huge increases in 'allowances'. That was on the premise that it would allow them to 'get out into their communities', and many a flock of pigs has been seen flying across the horizon ever since.

I have been involved with local councils for over thirty years, first as a councillor and then on the press bench and there is one area that is constantly overlooked – static councillors. Currently district and borough councillors serve four-year terms between elections after which they often stand for re-election. The result is too many of them hanging on for too many years, and that's bad news.

It has the effect of discouraging anyone else interested in being part of their local council, because usually the only available seats, in terms of being party political, are those usually seen to that particular party as being 'unwinnable'. Councillors holding the 'safe' seats usually see them as long term sinecures and stick to them, their original reasons for getting involved long forgotten.

So councils are regularly deprived of new talent and levels of enthusiasm that, if nurtured through experience, could even grace Parliament itself one day. What they get instead are the 'long-haulers', content to appear in public, spouting current party political theology once every four years, or tuck into the annual Civic Dinners with their spouses.

By and large, while there will always be exceptions, councillors are not corrupt; but the longer they are in power the more vulnerable in that sense they are. There is some occasional truth in the old saying about *'absolute power'*, and as a society we try to guard against it. The most effective way of doing so, and to ensure a regular supply of new blood coming into the council chamber, is to limit a councillor's time in office.

The President of the United States holds the most powerful political job in the world – but only for two four-year terms. Surely, what's good for Clinton and George W...etc, should be good enough for Cllr United Kingdom.

Some senior councillors will protest that it would mean the loss of all their experience, which would be true – but only in political terms. As in Government, the real work is done by the civil service anyway and its council officers who have the real experience, as well as the actual knowledge, of how the machine works.

This need not stop them standing for re-election – four years after their end of their second term gave someone else a chance, and even George W doesn't have that option. Certainly it would open more doors to frustrated would-be councillors who are denied the chance of a realistic shot at becoming a councillor – perhaps even of being Prime Minister one day.

The real winners would be democracy, local councils, and the people.

32

STORY

One for the grave

LADY WINCHELL FOUND DEAD – the stark black words burned themselves deep into Jackie Warren's horrified and disbelieving brain. If he had been feeling bad before, he was suddenly a thousand times worse now.

In a daze he fumbled in his pockets for a coin and, hands barely under control, thrust it at the newspaper vendor. He was convinced the man was staring at him, and thought he could see some glimmering of recognition in his eyes? Warren snatched the paper and stumbled away.

As a rising young criminal, he had sneered at the old lags who'd lost their bottle. Now, the veteran of several periods as a guest of Her Majesty himself, he knew what it was like. A compulsive thief, these days he too suffered agonies of fear after every job, always expecting the knock on the door that would herald the arrival of the Old Bill, yet unable to change his way of life and go straight.

Since he'd come out of HMP Chelmsford after his last stretch the state of his nerves, made ragged by the fear of going back, had got progressively worse. It had seemed even more so since last night's job. His whole body was shaking uncontrollably, and his stomach felt like a bouncy castle with a hundred kids shouting and jumping up and down in it.

He'd been awake all night with his shattered nerves making sleep impossible. The agonising cramps in his stomach had been bad enough – they had certainly not prepared him for the headline that had stared him in the face outside that morning. His mind in turmoil, Jackie leaned heavily on a nearby shop window desperately trying to get his mind straight enough to sort things out.

They may not hang murderers any more, yet he imagined he could feel the course hemp around his throat, cutting deep into his sweaty neck. He gasped and gulped for air, as a thousand jumbled thoughts jostled through his confused brain. He knew, as he stood there shaking and trembling in the street, that he was drawing attention to himself. Yet he was rooted to the spot, transfixed – the newspaper whose words had unleashed the reign of terror in his brain, held tightly in his hand. This time, he knew, they would throw away the key.

Somewhere deep inside that brain, the instincts of self-preservation finally began to drag him back to the reality of the moment. Clearly he could not stay where he was, because every copper on the manor knew him, and was probably looking for him now. He had to get away from there, and fast.

Had it been a simple case of robbery, things might have been very different. Even though the victim was an old lady, it probably wouldn't have meant a great deal to the plod in Ilford. The sight of a Romford villain, even in an excitable condition, probably would not have been connected to a job done off his patch. Murder, though, that was different – that was a bird of a very different feather. 'Bird?' Even that casual thought set him shaking again, reminding him of that waiting cell – one which this time would be part of a long term residence.

He had to move. Thrusting the newspaper into a pocket in his jacket Warren forced his unwilling limbs into action. Through the fog of his mind, all his instincts told him that in the state he was in, public transport was not a good idea. He'd be bound to be remembered by someone on a bus or train. He would quite literally have to get up on his toes, and quickly.

He broke into a run, trying to give the impression he was racing for a bus or train. He hoped it might even cool down the

Still In My Own Lynchtime

cheeks he could feel burning like hell, or perhaps relax the grip of the steel vice still clamping his stomach. As he hurried through the streets, his fevered brain was still trying to make some sense of what had happened.

"I never laid a finger on 'er. Well, except when I nicked the brooch!" he moaned to himself, desperately searching his memory as he hurried along. For a brief second or two he brightened up at the possibility that the old girl might actually have had a heart attack, or fallen over in a drunken stupor cracking her head open all by herself.

But desperation was doing the thinking for him now but, even as the thought crossed his shattered mind, he was already dismissing it as unlikely. If the forensics people could put him in the flat, as logic was telling him they would, he knew he'd carry the can – even if the old girl had popped her clogs by accident.

"Oh Gawd, 'ow did I ever get into this one?" A passer-by who heard Jackie's words, as he paused and leaned heavily gasping for breath against a wall, looked curiously at him – unsure whether to offer help or to avoid this man acting so oddly.

The old girl had seemed like a gift from the gods, at the time. He'd come across her by pure chance, standing behind her in the off-licence he'd popped into for a packet of fags. He couldn't even remember why he'd been in Ilford that day; but he was certainly struck by the huge wad of folding money she'd flashed to buy two bottles of Bells whisky. He'd hardly been able to take his greedy little eyes off it – and the fact that most of it now rested in his own wallet of course, was the cause of all his problems.

Since she seemed to be eighty if she was a day, Jackie had made a joke of it after holding the door open so the old girl could totter out of the shop. "She ain't under age, is she? he'd laughed as the shopkeeper served him afterwards.

The geyser had grinned a response. "Who, milady?" he'd chuckled as he put Jackie's cigarettes onto the counter. He told Jackie that the old girl was his best customer – regular as clockwork, and who turned up every morning for her couple of bottles of Scotch.

"She's a widow and she really is a Lady. Her name's Lady Winchell, and she lives over there with a couple of cats", he nodded towards a very clearly up-market block of apartments on the opposite side of the street. "I guess she likes her booze, and long may she do so as far as I am concerned", he'd added as he handed over Jackie's change.

That had been a week ago – a week in which Jackie had made a few discreet enquiries about the old lady. Her old man had been a 'Sir' something or other, and had left her pots of dosh years ago, and ever since he'd fallen off the twig, his widow had been steadily drinking her way through it. Seems she wasn't keen on banks, so clearly had plenty of the stuff washing around, and what about the jewellery? She must have had some quality tom up there in her pad as well.

It had been easier to get into the place than even Jackie had thought it would be. They might have been exclusive apartments, with security and all the rest of it all, but security men who support Arsenal do tend to be a little bit on the slack side when the Gunners playing Newcastle is on the telly. As for the front door of Lady Winchell's own flat – well, that was no match for a man who had spent years sharing cells with some of the best lock pickers in the business.

It had taken him only a few seconds to get inside, and the scene that greeted him there was delightful for his purpose. The old girl was paralytic – stoned out of her mind, barely conscious, and slumped in an armchair in the living room. An open half empty bottle of Scotch was on the table, with an empty glass beside it. Another bottle – this one very empty – had fallen to the floor at her feet much earlier in the day.

Though she was clearly out of things, Lady Winchell was just about conscious. Despite her befuddled state she knew he was there, but she was so drunk she could hardly speak, let alone take in the significance of his being there. But she did try.

"Yesh? "Who are you? Whatdya want?" she had slurred before collapsing back into her chair in fits of hysterical laughter. Stupid old cow!

She was so completely out of it she made no protest as he rifled through her purse, relieving her of the strain of carrying that heavy load of paper that had attracted his attention in the first place. She'd even helped him to a bonus.

"What about thish...?" She'd cackled, pointing the diamond brooch pinned to her scraggy chest. The pin had been a bit difficult, and he'd ended up practically tearing it off her dress as she fell back into the chair, and drifted off back into that deep alcoholic doze she had been woken from.

Those loud snores had been a comfort to the thief as he moved swiftly and easily around the flat, ransacking it and helping himself to bits and pieces he could carry and that he knew he'd be able to fence easily. As long as he could hear her snoring he felt free to roam through the place, plundering it without worrying too much.

After he'd reckoned he'd finished, he'd gone back to the chair for one last look at the old bat Standing over 'Milady's' slumbering body, he picked up the bottle, poured another large measure of the whisky and put the glass back onto the table beside her, before straightening up again.

"Here you go, darlin! You'll need that when you wake up" he'd laughed. Then, he raised the bottle with a mocking gesture to her health, before taking a good long swig from it himself. Then he'd grinned and screwed the cap back onto it before sliding the bottle into his pocket for later. His victim was still snoring like a sawmill as he moved towards the door, and out into the corridor. Downstairs the security men had still been engrossed in the Arsenal game on the telly.

Happy Jackie

Jackie had been a happy man as he'd walked back down the street that afternoon. He'd got a right result and all he needed to do now was to fence the tom and he was quids in, as well as having the cash he'd nicked from her. It was at that point that the sudden thought struck him. Without warning he stopped in his tracks – forcing a young mother pushing her pram behind him to 'tut tut' her impatience as she wheeled it around him.

"Oh my Gawd – the glass?" That old familiar panic began to pulsate in his stomach. Frantically he tried to remember whether he had kept the gloves on, or had he taken them off, to pour the old girl that last stupid glass of whisky. Was that final act of mockery going to backfire and point a finger directly at him? He groaned, causing a few more passers by to look curiously at him as they hurried by.

It had been that sort of clumsiness that had put him in the dock so many times before. Idiotic, juvenile, and deadly mistakes that almost always opened up a prison cell as far as he was concerned. Now the fear and foreboding was starting to become a conviction that he'd blundered yet again. He couldn't be sure, but even the possibility was churning him up inside, as he rushed back to his tatty little Romford bedsit.

By the time he'd reached it and slammed the door behind him he was a mental wreck. Yes, he could clearly remember keeping his gloves on all through his visit. Yes, he could remember just as clearly taking them off to pour that bloody drink...or had he? He just didn't know – one minute he thought he hadn't, and the next was more convinced that he had.

He'd spent a wretched night anxiously anticipating the knock on the door he was certain would come. At least he had Lady Winchell's bottle for company, or at least what was left of it, because the worse he felt the more he needed. As the evening had turned into night, and then into to the early hours of the morning, the demons inside him had not been calmed down by the Scotch – indeed they'd got worse.

After a couple more glasses he'd even given that up and tried to sleep. It proved to be impossible – he tossed and turned, sweating and shaking all night, the clamps of fear grinding away inside his body, made worse by the deathly prospect of more porridge, made any thought of sleep impossible.

He'd been relieved to see the dawn come, with still no knock on the door, but by lunchtime things were no better physically or mentally – even though there was still no sign of the constabulary. The idea of food was the last thing on his mind, but he was desperate for something to soothe those demons, and the fact no copper had arrived to ask questions, had given him some degree of confidence. He knew he had to risk it. It was as he left Boots with some tummy calming jollop in his hand that he'd seen that awful newspaper headline.

Still In My Own Lynchtime

Now he knew for sure that by now that forensics would have been all over her flat. This was murder, and they would be leaving no stone unturned. All the questions and doubts in his mind about whether or not he'd left his prints on that glass, resurfaced. He knew they would lead directly to Romford, and that imaginary noose seemed to get ever tighter around his neck, choking him and making the whole of his head thud with the pain.

Suddenly he realised he was in a part of Romford he didn't know – in which case it was safe to assume that no one knew him there either. He felt a little safer and relaxed slightly, desperately trying to think through the pain, which was still racking his body. A drink, yes that was it! He needed a drink – the hair of the dog – anything that would calm his tattered nerves and perhaps still his fluttering limbs.

He was pushing open a door. The name of the pub never mattered – as he staggered to the bar he neither knew nor cared. "Large scotch!" his voice was dry and croaking, as he demanded the drink.

The barmaid turned away to pick up a glass, before holding it beneath the optic to let the amber liquid flow into it. Her neat figure and long red hair would have normally have attracted more attention from Jackie Warren, but he was beyond all that. He could barely see her through the agonising mist in front of his eyes.

"You alright, sir", She asked, as she took the coins he had practically thrown down onto the bar. Ignoring her, he picked the drink up and steered an unsteady course to a table in a distant and isolated corner.

The whisky didn't help very much – it certainly never settled his stomach or stopped the trembling or sweating. In fact, if anything he was feeling worse than before, but he steeled himself to look natural before taking the newspaper out of his pocket to read the story properly. The words in front of him were a blur, while all around him the whole room swirled more and more out of focus, but somehow he managed to summon the strength to concentrate on words he could hardly focus on.

It seems the old lady's Home Help had found her dead in the

chair when she'd arrived to clean up the flat that day, and had called the police.

The reminder, and the reference to the coppers, renewed the waves of agony racking through Jackie's body. The paper shook as his hands convulsed even harder, and the words got hazier and more indistinct – but somehow he forced himself to press on to the last swirling and increasingly hazy paragraph.

'A police spokesman revealed they had found a suicide note in Lady Winchell's handwriting. They had also found an empty whisky bottle and a glass of whisky, which had been tested and found to contain a massive and lethal dose of barbiturates', the report finished.

・・・・・・

The barmaid watched sympathetically as the paramedics carried the blanket-covered body out to their ambulance and on their way to the hospital mortuary.

"I didn't think he looked very well when he came in. Then he just sort of, gave a strangled cry and collapsed in a heap", she told anyone nearby who happened to be listening.

Jackie Warren wasn't listening, though.

33

Dagenham Posted

Heroes, for a handful of marbles

First we had the Dandy and the Beano, and thrilled to the antics of Korky the Cat, Desperate Dan (with his cow pies) and Denis the Menace. Every week we saw the misadventures of Laurel and Hardy in Film Fun, and Arthur Askey in Radio Fun. Well, it was a distraction from the air raid sirens.

Then one day we infants became pupils at the junior school in Stevens Road and began to put away our childish comics, for some more serious reading in the Hotspur, Wizard, Champion and Rover. Our role models now were no longer Julius Sneezer – the Roman Geezer – and Lord Snooty and his pals. No, now we had some new comic book heroes.

Yes, we had Dick Barton every weekday evening on the wireless, and Roy Rogers or Hopalong Cassidy at the Saturday Morning Pictures, and very good they were too – but they had serious competition. Our most regular heroes had names like Cannonball Kidd, Alf Tupper, Rockfist Rogan and the 'greatest athlete of all time', Wilson.

For most of us urchins, fame and stardom was a far and distant dream though for some of us local kids, like Dudley Moore, Jimmy Greaves and Terry Venables, it became a reality, and out of jealously we hated them for it. No, we lived our heroics through our serious comics – or the occasional American one that somehow contrived to arrive on the street's swapping market.

To us Rockfist Rogan was what Biggles had been in the first war, in terms of being a flying 'ace', but he also had a pretty mean left hook when it came to the noble art of course. Strictly a Marquess of Queensbury rules man of course, no week went by when after blasting the odd Stuka out of the sky, he pulled out his boxing gloves from behind his Spitfire seat and found some low life to beat up.

Alf Tupper – the 'Tough of the Track' – was another great favourite with us. There were no pretensions about working class Alf, who ran a welding business under some railway arches, between pulling on some cheap spikes and ragged running vest to show a clean pair of heels to some snobby public school runners.

Cannonball Kidd was a teenage centre forward who joined up with a famous old team after the war, in which they'd lost their own centre forward veteran. Week after week Cannonball would score the vital winning goal of course and year after year they won the cup and the league championship. Another footballing hero was 'Baldy Hogan', whose team had a colour-blind goalkeeper, a problem they solved by having RAF roundels printed on the back and front of their shirts. Yes, I know – but they preceded Roy of the Rovers by years, and always played the decent chaps who never cheated, swore or played dirty. We idolised our kitchen table heroes, and in honesty tried to live the way they lived.

We loved our stars and passed them and their adventures around the street in barter and exchange deals, sometimes also involving marbles or cigarette cards. For us they were streets ahead of Superman and Captain Marvel – though to be fair we never turned our noses up at them either.

Anyway we had our British 'superman' – your average 200-year old hermit who had emerged from the Yorkshire moors and who, on a diet of roots and herbs could still out-run and out-jump anyone alive. With his high moral values and simple lifestyle, dear old Wilson was tops with us all. Virtuous, celibate, abstemious and philosophical, it could be that he hadn't been in hibernation for two centuries – probably just seemed like it.

34

Dagenham Posted

A bootful of beer

It was Bob Davis who had the idea – or at least who picked up the mess deck buzz that led us to rolling out the barrel in a brewery.

It was sheer coincidence that we'd met in the first place. I was one of three National Service matelots being drafted out of Chatham to join the MTB base (HMS Hornet) in Gosport. We had a leading stoker (we all became renamed Engineer Mechanics months later) in charge of us as we headed for Hampshire, and on the train he revealed that he also came from Dagenham. Even more so his father was a bus inspector and mine was a bus driver – both of them working out of Seven Kings garage at that time.

Needless to say Bob and I became travelling companions (he lived in Bennetts Castle Lane – about a hundred yards from our place in Becontree Avenue) whenever we got weekend or long leaves.

Although Bob was nearing the end of his twelve years as a regular, like most sailors he was perpetually skint – a state even more so when it came to us National Heroes on 28bob (less than £1.50) a week. So as we were going home for a couple of weeks summer leave, he asked if I was interested in making a few bob by doing some casual work, I jumped at the idea.

I was even more enthusiastic when he said it would be in a brewery – well, you would, right? It turned out that he'd heard about a brewery in Whitechapel, which was always keen to offer casual (cash in hand) work to servicemen on leave. All we needed to do was be there by 8am, and a day or so later Bob and I were on a 7am 25 bus to Aldgate.

When we arrived there was already a number of young, fit and clearly active young men with the dead giveaway haircuts waiting outside. Dead on time a bloke came out of the brewery with a handful of discs in his hand, shouting that he needed fifteen men. Bob and I got the discs that signalled we were 'in'. It was surely a matelot's dream – we were going to work in a brewery.

Most of the lads were army and a few RAF types but the common denominator was that we were all servicemen, and apart from Bob, doing our National Service, and we were to be the 'chain gang'. This meant we were to be the 'muscle' that shifted full barrels of beer from one part of the brewery to the warehouse from where it would be picked up by the draymen to cart all over the local pubs.

Now some of those barrels were massive jobs that really did need some strength to roll them in straight lines (you try it sometime). In fact some of these barrels seemed to be under the impression that they were in fact supermarket trolleys with minds of their own.

Our favourites were the little firkins, because they could be 'bowled' along 'Drake style' to each other as we waited in line. Dead easy job really – no brain needed, which was just as well since only Bob and I were navy (ahem).

All went well and then, about an hour or so after we'd started, an old bloke appeared among us clutching a half pint glass in one hand, and a clearly full watering can without a spray on the end of the spout in the other.

'Have you had your beer?' he asked, before filling the glass with mild ale and handing it to each of us in turn. In fact he asked us several times and was always assured we hadn't, so he obliged us with more glassfuls all morning. Not, I grant you, the most hygienic way to take your booze – but it was free booze, after all, and by lunchtime we were all feeling pretty relaxed and happy.

We all went to the canteen for lunch and there all the full time workers, old boys close to retirement to a man, sat around playing cards and chatting. We, the nation's defenders of our country were all flaked out on our backs on benches.

After lunch it was the same routine – pushing and shoving barrels, bowling the little ones along, but all of us with hangovers from the morning beer – a company treat which was not repeated in the afternoon.

By five o'clock we were all shattered – bones creaking and muscles we never even knew we had aching like mad and giving us real gip. However, we all perked up a bit when the overseer came back and thrust some paper money into our hands in exchange for our discs.

A couple of days later though, Bob Davis decided he'd had enough and would spend the rest of his leave in Dagenham, rather than the brewery. I had very little choice, being permanently skint of course. A few days into my second week though, tragedy struck.

During our firkin bowling sessions one of the army lads got a bit bored with the Francis Drake bit and decided that Ted Drake might be more appropriate – Ted of course being one of the great centre forwards of our parents day. It proved to be a great variation and we took to our new game with gusto – until one of us put his foot through the end of one of the firkins.

Even worse, it was me and as a couple of quarts of best Indian Pale Ale gushed out all over my boot, the overseer appeared again – and this time he wasn't best pleased and nor did he see the funny side. He sacked the entire chain gang on the spot and left us in no doubt that our brewery careers were over.

It was great while it lasted though, and once our bones and muscles had got used to the exercise we were able to cope with it – and the free booze – quite well, but I guess the biggest downside was going home to Dagenham on the 25.each evening. There, despite it being rush hour, other passengers set up an exclusion zone around us.

Well, to be fair we did smell like a brewery.

35

Dagenham Posted

The happiest days of my life? No way!

I suppose, from a safe distance of sixty or so years, Stevens Road was no worse than any other school of its day; but kids now seem to think they are being hard done by if they have to hand in their mobile phones during lessons. They don't know the half of it. For me, school days were definitely not the happiest days of my life, either before or after Stevens Road.

It was a school built for the new LCC overspill Becontree estate on which we lived, and consisted of infant, junior and senior schools. The estate itself was a massive development which covered parts of both 'posh' Tory-voting Ilford and 'definitely working class' Socialist Dagenham.

Though our part of the Avenue was in Ilford, we definitely came into the Dagenham category. It was easy to tell the difference – we in the Ilford part had electric street lamps in our part of the Avenue, while across the border (Bennett's Castle Lane) in Dagenham they still had gas lamps.

We had moved into 349 Becontree Avenue in 1940 – a matter of weeks before the Luftwaffe redistributed our old house in Telham Road (a stone's throw from West Ham's ground – but I think they were probably aiming at the docks rather than Upton Park). I was five by then, so it was a case of 'new house new school', though it was my first one.

Still In My Own Lynchtime

I remember when my own children started school they, and apparently all the other kids of their age, actually looked forward to it. We certainly didn't.

The gates of Stevens Road Infant School were jammed with screaming five-year olds that day, hanging on to their mums for dear life and grizzelling as teachers almost dragged us into school so the mums could escape. The fact is that attitudes and teaching methods have changed quite dramatically. In our day and environment school was more often seen as that dreadfully boring period between playtime and going home. Without exception my pals and I hated school from the start.

Of course it didn't help much when some pretty important plasticine sculpting, (in the Infants), was being constantly interrupted by our Luftwaffe visitors popping over on their way to reshape London. At such times we were promptly marched into the air raid shelter − a brick built windowless building not even underground like our Anderson at home in the garden was. In the Junior school a year or so later, many a crucial marbles or cigarette-card tournament was seriously jeopardised by some German pratt in France who had aimed one of his doodlebugs in our general direction.

As far as the V2 rockets were concerned − it never mattered because they were blowing people up before the air raid sirens even had a chance to start up and let you know about it. The doodlebugs were different. You not only heard them coming from a long way off, you heard their engines stop and held your breath for ten seconds or so. You only breathed again when you heard the bang that signaled that someone else wouldn't be.

I suppose it would be easy to blame the war for the fact that we all had short personal fuses too. Few 'playtimes' went by without the magic word 'Fight! Fight!' sweeping around the playground. Immediately everyone stopped kicking balls about, hopscotching or, in the case of the girls skipping or doing handstands up against a wall with their dresses tucked into their knickers, to rush over to where the 'bundle' was already gathering an audience.

It was an established routine. Two scruffy short trousered urchins, socks collapsed around ankles, circled each other muttering threats and invitations for the other one to dare to make the first move.

"Yeah?"

"Yeah!"

"Well come on then."

"Nah, you come on – why doncha try it?"

It got a bit boring after a while, and reduced members at ringside to start shouting for one or the other to 'do im'. Suddenly one would hurl himself into the arms of his enemy, to the roars and shrieks of the audience – particularly from the girls who always thrust themselves to the front to see better, in the hope that blood might flow.

There they would see the two scruffs on the ground and wrestling like mad, rolling over and over on the gravel, each trying to create damage on the other while keen to avoid it themselves. There was a lot of grunting and groaning – but very little actual blood involved at first.

The main tactic was to get on top and sit, legs astride the one beneath, and gripping both his wrists. Now, at this point the kid on top would run out of ideas, because if he let go one wrist to thump his victim he stood a pretty good chance of getting whacked himself.

The one thing we never did was 'put the boot in'. We fought with our fists and arms – never with the boots, and I think it is a shame that in that sense we were perhaps more civilized than some of today's generations.

The battle itself would usually come to a finish with the arrival of duty playground teacher, usually a 'Miss' because most of the blokes were in the army. She'd been disturbed from the quiet cuppa she'd been enjoying in the staff room, so she was usually pretty miffed over the noise and chaos that had caused her to be called out.

It would end in a melee of teacher's hands dragging the ragamuffins apart, and marching them off to stand outside the headmistresses study. The cheated ringsiders would be lined up in their classes ready to be marched back in again. The 'action men' – neither of whom would blame the other for starting the ruckus of course – were usually 'slippered' or rapped over the

Still In My Own Lynchtime

knuckles with a ruler. All part of a days schooling, in Stevens Road Junior school.

We'd learned to live with all that, because it the way of things – but the most outstanding difference between then and now was the teaching itself. None of your electronic gadgetry, calculators or computers – no virtual reality tours of Agincourt of course. What we had was down-to-earth brainwashing by numbers – spelling bees, mental arithmetic and mass recitations – in classes that never dipped below the 55 mark in the register.

We recited everything from Sea Fever to the 'three times' table, either as a solo performance in front of the class at the behest of 'miss', or as a communal exercise by the massed tongues and tonsils of the whole class. We chanted on demand everything from the Lord's Prayer to 'Good Morning Miss So-and-so', like a well-rehearsed chorus line, at the drop of a well-aimed piece of chalk.

Yet we would also be the lucky generation. We had the war and rationing yes, but we were also had the free milk and Virol, the Butler Act which decreed that all the nation's little rascals should have the blessing of a free education up to the age of 15, and Bevan's NHS which looked after our physical well being. Pity none of us appreciated it much at the time.

In fact we did have the advantages of some great technological and social advances our parents never had. They'd never had much in the way of paper and pencils – and dad in particular had learned his sums and spelling with chalk and slate boards. As far as other differences were concerned my father had certainly gone to his Catholic school in Wapping during the First World War, many times without benefit of shoes or boots on his feet.

I had always been doubtful on that claim until one day I saw a photo in a book on East End poverty of his day in which all the were ragged and barefoot. We always had boots or shoes – with 'blakey's' or steel studs in them to help make the soles and heels last longer and made us sound like the third act of Lullaby of Broadway as we ran down the street.

I drifted through Stevens Road Junior, with the celebratory days off VE and VJ and only a couple of playground punch-ups over disputed cigarette cards about the only things that really marked it out. Then I made one of my life's great blunders – I only went and passed 'the scholarship'.

Ostracised by the Mild Bunch

Once we neared the age of 11 we had to 'sit the scholarship', as the eleven-plus was called then. Success in this exam qualified you either to go on to a grammar, technical or other form of 'high school', though it was often simply called 'going to college'.

For me, failure would have meant the Stevens Road Senior School, which had all the beckoning allure of taking the first dead end job that came along when you reached working age. (Unless you were lucky enough to get an apprenticeship somewhere) There was a lifeline for those who reached 13 and hadn't made it the first time though. They were classified as 'late developers' and given one last opportunity to impress the high schools with their promise and thus qualify to go to one of them for their last few school years.

To be honest, at that stage I would have been happy as a van-boy – but no! I had to send Mum into deliriums of delight by doing what no one, even me, ever thought possible. I not only went and passed it first time at the age of 10.

My reward was that I had first choice. That was the South East Essex County Technical School in Longbridge Road, though for the first couple of years we had to go to Rosslyn Road, Barking, which was the junior part of the school.

Even Dad got over-emotional – well, he did until he saw the list of requirements that came with the scholarship – uniforms, pens and pencils, and satchels full of sports gear. For me, though, the worst thing that happened was being ostracized by the 'Mild Bunch'

I had grown up with Ginger Barratt, and 'Buddy' Blythe, along with a couple of others, during the war. We'd fought each other for the milkman's horse manure for Mum's tomatoes, snowballed and joined in stone fights against the gang from the next street (Winding Way). Yes, we really did hurl stones, and lumps of brick from a nearby bombsite, at each other when there was no snow about. We'd played street football with old and shiny tennis balls, and cricket using the street pig bins for a wicket. We'd hopscotched, marbled, and ambushed many a redskin in 'the bushes' that ran down the centre of the avenue – but suddenly I was bad news. I was a 'college kid' and, in their eyes, a snob.

Even worse I had to go from the standard scruffy urchin kit of ragged pullover, stained jacket, and short trousers with hanging underpants – to blazer, grey flannel long trousers, white shirt and school tie, not forgetting that bloody cap. Even the shoes had to get used to a very regular, albeit unaccustomed, dab or two of Cherry Blossom followed by a vigorous brushing.

It all proved to be a bit of a false dawn as far as I was concerned. Within a few weeks of reaching the 'tech' I was clod of the month so often they could have built a golf course with my school reports. My only excuse was that because of the accident of my date of birth, I was about six months younger than any of my classmates.

In fact, half way through my two years at Rosslyn Road, I was put back a year so suddenly I was half a year older than my new classmates. Didn't make a blind bit of difference! Mum and Dad were mystified. How could their oldest child, smart enough to win the scholarship at his first attempt, turn out to be about as useful as a luminous sundial 'in college'?

Algebra? Geometry? Logarithms? I had trouble even spelling them, and as for languages, well, it was a good job the war was over before I could become an RAF fighter pilot ace. The amount of German Mrs (Frau) Morrison – a Jewish lady of German extraction who had fled to this country before the war – managed to cram into me would not have got me into Stalag Luft 3, let alone out of it. Mind you, Mrs M did have other unforgettable tendencies.

Apart from a thick guttural accent, she was built like the proverbial barn door, with hands like shovels; she also had a very neat line in blackboard ear-thumping. Upset her, and she would carefully position you alongside the wall blackboard before giving you a pretty hefty clout around the ear that sent your head bouncing off the board. Since this was only a few years after the war, you can imagine what we called this lady and how much we speculated on who'd trained her, and where.

English wasn't much better either – in fact the only reason I developed a passing command of it was down more to the Hotspur and Wizard comics, than to the sad post-war parade of recently demobbed and frustrated novelists they employed to teach us.

Still, you know what they say about English. If at first you don't succeed...quit, and become a journalist.

36

Dagenham Posted

Music was not my food of love

One of the great sadnesses I have in life is that although I grew up in a house which had its own piano – regularly dusted and polished – in the 'best' or front room, I never got much further on it than a hesitant one-fingered version of God Save the King (as we had then).

I suppose my other claim to musical fame is that I was a member of the Valence House library at the same time as Dudley Moore was, and we walked home together a couple of times. As far as musical appreciation in general was concerned, that was slightly inhibited by some German 'clout', and Fat Mary of 2C who came between Mozart and me.

Our piano spent its days largely as a family ornament – a highly polished dust-trap whose top served as a shelf, upon which rested framed photos of Mum and Dad's wedding and a coloured glass bowl which only ever saw active service at Christmas when it held nuts.

The keyboard part of the piano only saw action on those sort of rare occasions when we had something to celebrate and had parties. Mum came into her own then, because she was the only one in the family who could get any kind of recognisable tune out of it. She couldn't read a note of music, but she could belt out a tune on the ivories.

So at Christmas, VE and VJ-days and the odd birthday bash, she would be pressed into sitting down at the 'Joanna', and soon had all the aunts and uncles singing about Mother Macrae, taking Kathleen home again, or that real party pooper 'We'll meet again' – which left everyone so emotional they couldn't sing any more anyway.

I can see Dad to this day, half-empty glass of brown ale in hand, leaning on the top of the piano, almost with tears pouring down his face as he slurred the words about that dear old land 'across the Irish Sea' Which was a bit strong for a Wapping cockney lad whose only experience of crossing water had been on the Woolwich free ferry or Tower Bridge, though to be fair he did have Irish ancestors.

There were some memorable musical moments though. Not long after VE day for instance, we had a street party where all us kids had fishpaste sandwiches followed by jelly and blanc mange, washed down with lemon barley water. Meanwhile the adults poured copious amounts of brown ale and shandies down their throats as they sang like the bunch of drunks they were that day.

Our piano was out of the best room into the street and Mum was thumping away at the patriotic throat-catchers like 'There'll always be an England' along the highly cultural tunes like 'Knees up Mother Brown' as the street partied, and burnt anything that the Luftwaffe hadn't already burnt on a massive bonfire in the middle of the road.

Sadly, Mum never passed on her musical talent to me, though I did make a tentative start, at the age of six. I was the 'lead triangle' in the Stevens Road Infants Percussion Band, but that was about it. There were odd moments of musical culture to come, like a few years later at the 'Tech', when I helped form the 3C3 'paper and comb' washroom combo.

That broke up after we got a detention because we had been so absorbed in our own interpretation of 'She'll Be Coming Round the Mountain When She Comes', that we'd totally forgotten about the biology lesson we should have been involved in.

There were some opportunities to acquire some appreciation

Still In My Own Lynchtime

of music at the Tech though. While doing our first couple of years in the Rosslyn Road (Barking) part of the school, apart from music lessons, we had the regular concerts by the legendary Barking Quintet.

Our music teacher, Miss Shepherd, was a meek little soul who was totally out of her depth in the teaching business and we played her unmercifully. Her only means of keeping control of our kind of uncultured scruffs was to despatch the unruly to report to her friend, Mrs Morrison, the German teacher. Mrs M was a huge German-born lady whose guttural English made her sound even more formidable to us, bearing in mind this was barely a couple of years after the war.

Rumour had it that she had been one of the Jewish refugees who had fled from Hitler's unfriendly society during the thirties, had married over here but had lost her husband during the war. Now she was teaching us her native language and, as far as we were concerned, she was not nice people – possibly because half of us couldn't understand half what she was saying most of the time.

As I said, this was not long after the end of the war and we kids all had some less than fond memories of Germans, and that wasn't helped by some of the revelations that were still coming out at the time. Because the 'fearsome Frau' was German and, in our eyes a bully, you can imagine where we speculated that she had been trained. Believe me, this lady did not take prisoners.

So Miss Shepherd knew exactly what she was doing when she sent us over to her friend. We, the naughty ones playing up, would soon be trooping one by one across the quadrangle to Mrs Morrison's class, timidly entering to a chorus of giggling from a class relieved at yet another interruption to their German lesson. They knew, and we knew, we were about to be beaten up for their entertainment.

The old cow would look up and glare as we opened the classroom door and nervously approached. She would gesture us to stand to the side of her, sideways on to the wall-blackboard. Very often there was already a line of our own classmates facing the wall.

"Vat are you here for?" She already knew why and we hardly

got the words out that Miss Shepherd had sent us over, before she spat out 'Vy?' We would start to stammer we had been messing about a bit, but even as we did her beefy right hand was already sweeping up with unerring accuracy to clump us on the side of the face.

The blow sent the head jerking right onto the blackboard she had positioned us against, bouncing off just in time to catch the next right-hander, on its way up. Then, still seeing stars and listening to bells ringing in our ears, we were gestured to join the line-up and wait for the next victim to be evicted by Miss S.

Still, despite the pain and shock, even that was a bit of a relief from the crochets and semi-quavers Miss Shepherd was failing sadly to inspire any kind of enthusiasm about music into us. But, we also had the Barking Quintet.

This was a strolling band of musical worthies who had a contract with schools in Barking. They had the near impossible task of shoving some sort of musical and cultural appreciation of 'posh' music, into what were effectively street-rakers straight off the bombsite playgrounds.

Most of us found them about as welcome as toothache, but these were command performances – by command of Miss Coleman, the headmistress. She was determined that we would enjoy the delights of Mozart and learn to appreciate the finer points of the violin, viola, and bass etc. To be honest – no chance!

On Quintet days, each class was marched in an orderly fashion across the quadrangle, and into the dinner hall cum assembly hall.. There we would sit cross-legged on the splintery parquet floor staring miserably at the empty chairs, music stands, violin cases and big bass fiddle, at the front. We would be shushed as the members of the group filed in, presumably having been liberally entertained in Miss Coleman's office. As they made themselves comfortable and ready for their recital, our teachers legged it, and left us to it.

By the time the lead violinist had started his chat about Mozart, Brahms or whoever, most of the staff were living it up well out of earshot in the staff-room. Only a few eagle eyed music appreciators like Miss Shepherd of course, were left to pick up on any of us not paying attention. The up-side was that, provided you were sitting at the back of the hall, or hunched up behind someone like 'Fat Mary' of 2C2 you could read the Hotspur in peace, with little fear of having it confiscated and copping a detention. Certainly no trips across the quad to the Fearsome Frau were on offer.

Nowadays I enjoy music very much and of all kinds – even the 'posh' stuff. Being raised on Anne Ziegler and Webster Booth, the Andrew Sisters, Vera Lynn and Bud Flanagan however, was no real preparation for Sibelius, Shostakovitch or Grieg. A few years further on and dance music – ballroom or jazz – would be a very necessary part of our lives for the bird-pulling Saturday nights at the Ilford Palais and Broad Street baths. At the time of the Quintet though, we post-war scruffs then had all the musical appreciation of a forklift truck.

We may have been the generation that, a few years later, launched Rock n Roll, but the Barking Quintet never had us bopping in the aisles the way Bill Haley and Buddy Holly would. No one – as far as I know – has ever rioted or ripped up the seats in Covent Garden's Royal Opera House after getting carried away by the likes of Verdi or the voice of Pavarotti.

Mind you some small nods of music appreciation were beginning to penetrate our skulls. Jazz, Jolson and Glenn Miller were already heroes to some of us, even before Hollywood started to rewrite their life stories, and soon your Frankie Laines and Guy Mitchells would be going on about Ghost Riders and Red Feathers on gramophones that usually reached us via some pretty dubious routes.

But as far as our musical education went, your Bach and Beethoven, Brahms (and not forgetting Liszt of course), were probably set back years as a result of having culture thrust upon us by the well-meaning and very sincere skills of 'the quintet', who were decidedly not into playing 'urchin' music.

If music really was the food of love, then we would have preferred something with chips in our dinner hall, thanks very much. Fat Mary of 2C2 certainly would have – bless her.

37

Dagenham Posted

Swimming on a parquet floor

Life had got a bit dull – the Blitz was over and we were in that 'quiet' period before the doodlebugs and rockets got the sirens wailing again. So the announcement that school swimming lessons would begin, was quite exciting. Our first lessons would be held in the school itself, though there was one major drawback – Stevens Road never had a pool.

We would be required to have swimming costumes, and that caused a bit of a panic at home because I never had one. What I did have was a clutch of older cousins and eventually a family appeal produced an old costume – a girl's one that had to be suitably re-designed by Mum.

Anyway it was with a great deal of anticipation that we turned up at school one day complete with cozzies for our first lesson, and we were marched into the hall. That must have been a sight to behold – forty skinny boys and girls, lined up in ranks and most wearing make-do-and-mend costumes.

We were taken through the arms part of the breaststroke. We were taught how to put our hands together like we were saying prayers, shove them up to a point above our heads, and then bring them down apart in a wide sweep, back to the prayer position. No problem – within minutes we were all flailing around like a human wind-farm – or would have been, had they been invented.

Once we had the arm movements off to a fine art, we got to the legs bit, or should I say 'leg'. Like a flock of bony storks, we stood on one leg and did the frog with the other, making sure we got the right co-ordination between our arms and leg. Every so often we had to change legs, but we started to get pretty good at one-legged dry swimming.

This went on for some weeks – we must have had the only swimming lessons where splinters and filthy feet rather than splashes, were the result and topless girls never did much for eight year old boys anyway.

Finally came the great day. Clearly believing us to be strong enough dry swimmers, they crocodiled us down to the bus stop to catch the No25 to the baths.

This was the first time I had actually ever been in a swimming pool. It took my breath away and suddenly doing the breaststroke Long John Silver style wasn't so easy. There was also another point our school-hall swimming teacher had forgotten – how and when to breathe. A couple of smarting eyes and spluttering mouthfuls of chlorinated water seemed to take all the shine of swimming.

Even worse I was not the only boy in the class finding his knitted woolen costume was falling down. So, apart from one-legged breast stroke, we were now trying to do it one-handed as well, holding cozzie up with the other. Well, we were still a mixed class, after all.

It was a couple of years before I could actually swim in real water. On floors in halls, living rooms and lawns, I could swim like a fish, but it wasn't until I went to a school, the South East Tech, which had its own pool and a swimming teacher who could actually swim as well, that I learned to do it in real water. In fact I became quite a strong swimmer and competed successfully in a number of swimming gala competitions, particularly as a boy scout.

I must admit being a swimmer did come in very handy during my National Service, because the Navy rather liked to be sure we could survive in water for a while at least. So, clad in boiler suit and plimsolls we had to jump into a pool, swim three lengths and tread water for three minutes, before swimming another couple of lengths. Those who failed were doomed to swimming lessons for the rest of their service or until they had done it. For me the old parquet floor plunges had finally paid off.

They did a few years later too, when I was a ship's engineer in a cargo ship, the Southern Prince, anchored about half a mile off New Zealand waiting for a dock berth to clear so we could get into Auckland.

Some beers, a few bravado bets and, being officers, we had some clout. Four of us were swimming ashore before you could say 'ahoy there me hearties'. OK, so we had a boat with us to bring the beer and take us back again, but I still break out into a cold sweat when I read about people being taken by sharks in that part of the world.

We never had that sort of thing in Stevens Road.

38

SOAPBOX

Give us our game back!

Whatever the Chairman and his board may believe, as they talk about selling out to property developers, the 'ammers does not belong to them. Yes, in financial terms West Ham United FC may – but the traditions of the club belongs to me, my late father and grandfather, along with many many thousands of family generations like us.

It's ours, just as Manchester United, Arsenal, Aston Villa and so many other clubs are owned by the 'coloured scarves and rattle generations', who stood on their terraces often throughout bitter winters, to cheer on their heroes. There were no rich Yanks, Russians or mystery Iranians standing in the cold with us then. What we had were just honest to goodness, often disparaged, British football club chairmen and directors, whose personal devotion to their local club was often a drain on their wallets.

Yes things have changed, and admittedly sometimes for the better. No longer do we have to relieve ourselves in stinking corrugated iron urinals at half time, or chew gristly meat pies wrapped in greaseproof paper, washed down with a cup of hot Bovril to keep the cold out. Nowadays we pay to get in with plastic or paper pledges, rather than hard earned coins – and youngsters no longer get 'air lifted' above heads down to the front, in Upton Park's legendary 'chicken run'.

Very obviously the game has changed on the field too. The only 'foreigners' in our teams had names beginning with 'Mc'. 'O', or they came out of the Welsh coalfields to express themselves, and we cheered them. The Macaulays, O'Farrells and the Woosnams were not Scots, Paddies and Taffys, they were 'ammers – the 'Irons' – just as Bermudian Clyde Best was when he helped open doors for black players in the British game.

Today our premier teams are packed with players with names we often can't pronounce, who speak with global tongues, and 'managed' by slick operators, keen to ensure their percentages are maintained.

Sometimes then we even travelled to the ground on the same bus as they did, but as we line up to go through the turnstiles today, they sweep past in their Ferraris into their own car park. We don't begrudge them their success, but it has created social barriers between the supporters and the players that never used to exist.

Yes, our top players were underpaid, often even by the standard of wage levels of the day; but can anyone really justify what we have to pay nowadays in order to justify exorbitant wages and transfer fees? Do we really need seasonal changes of strip, just so the club can squeeze as much cash out of their loyal fans as they can stand? Do we really need to re-mortgage in order to buy a season ticket?

Our loyalties are never in doubt – and never waver whatever the temptation. In January 1952 I cheered a personal hero, Stanley Matthews, when he visited Upton Park with Blackpool, but still celebrated when 'we' knocked his team out of the cup that day. Our generations have cheered them all, and 'advised' them when to pass or shoot. We've been proud of them all, from Syd Puddefoot and Dick Walker, to Bobby Moore and Trevor Brooking, because they were, and are, ours. We still do, whether we are at the game or just seeing them on Match of the Day.

Why? Because we are part of 'our club', whatever colours it plays in – just as the generations of Spurs, Arsenal, Manchester United etc fans are of theirs. We may be the forgotten army – a

Still In My Own Lynchtime

commercial milch cow – in the boardroom, but its one the 'owners' of the clubs would be tempting providence to take too much for granted. Without our support their investment comes down to the basics – real estate – and if we withdrew they would be left with some very hefty debts to service.

Football is a game played all over the country and still gives pleasure to those who love it, at whatever level its played – on local grounds and pitches, even in the park. Perhaps its time we took our game back!

Since writing this, WestHam has been bpght by an Icelandic biscuit maker – but he is at least a football man with a good soccer track record in his own country.

39

Dagenham Posted

On the run in the bushes

The 'Becontree' LCC estate was the result of a magnificent joint dream – by socialist politicians keen to empty the East End slums, and Henry Ford being just as keen to fill his new Dagenham plant assembly lines. While it is generally accepted as being Dagenham, in actual fact the estate extended way beyond the old 'village', even into Ilford and Barking with street after street of decent, if boring, houses that even had inside toilets and gardens.

Those architects included trees in the streets – even little 'copses' – and we had the parks, Goodmayes, Valence, Parsloes, etc. All of which meant our generation grew up in a better environment than our parents had, and in the Avenue we were even luckier because along our stretch we had 'the bushes'.

Starting at the Robin Hood (which I see has now gone but was where Dearly Beloved proposed to me), Becontree Avenue still stretches a few miles right down to Becontree Heath; but that couple of miles stretch is a dual carriageway with a wide strip of grass between the roads. In our day it wasn't grass – it was full of trees, bushes and shrubs, our own countryside. It was our Sherwood, our Burmese jungle trail and the woods through which we tracked the Sioux, depending what was on at the

Saturday morning pictures. It also helped us evade capture by Police Constable Lusher.

In our day that entire part of the Avenue, down to the Ilford/Dagenham border at Bennett's Castle Lane, was a long strip of woodland, full of trees and bushes of all varieties. Each local 'gang' of kids had its own hideout in the bushes and it was great. Within a few feet of our front doors we could climb trees, crawl through undergrowth to kill Japs, attack 'Indians', or ambush innocent pedestrians with a selection of weapons ranging from spud guns and catapults, to primitive bows and arrows. In fact it was that latter activity that got the Mild Bunch into trouble with P.C.Lusher...again, one day.

Living in a house a few doors from ours he knew us, and our parents, well and he was the bane of our young lives. It was Lusher who objected to our illuminating our guy as we begged in the gloom for pennies outside Jones; the newspaper shop in Green Lane, and made us blow out the candle on our barrow. A few weeks later he was complaining to our dads that we were tying bangers to people's doorknockers at night, and told them to confiscate the fireworks before he did, until November 5th.

This was the same 'honest cop', by the way, who once broke up the fight over the ownership of some fresh United Dairies horse-dung between Georgie Pickford and me. He sent us home with empty buckets to face irate mums who needed it for their gardens, while he nicked the damn stuff himself.

On this particular day he was just leaving his house to pedal off on his beat, when he spotted us hunting a big cat – well it looked big to us at the time – with a catapult. Problem was it was his cat, and he'd caught us bang to rights. Believe me, when Lusher shouted 'Oi!' you stopped and you listened.

Well, usually we did. This time we went up on our toes and scattered into the safety of 'the bushes' where we crawled under some of the deepest and thickest bushes there. Looking back on it, he probably knew roughly where we lay – even worse of course he knew us and where we lived. So we were caught between two stools – did we give ourselves up and get bashed over the head with his rolled up cycle cape again? Or did we stay in hiding, hoping he'd go away? We opted for cowardice, keeping our fingers crossed he wouldn't bring it up with our parents later. Which he did!

After the war, with more traffic on the roads, the bushes were a clear road safety problem, so they cut them all down and made it a lawn. So, if a Lusher ever rides again, (yeah, like the local plod rides push bikes these days) the scallywags have no hiding place.

EPILOGUE

In my own Lynchtime

The war was over – we were all safer now
The Luftwaffe could hurt us no more
It was time to live, to learn, and to grow
To play, to laugh, to shout and to roar

These were the years of our youth
And we talk about them still
OK so we're now longer in the tooth
But we're not yet quite over the hill

We were boys, and they will always be boys
Playing football and cricket in the park
We made our own joyful kind of noise
Scoring winning runs and great goals until dark

In our teens we discovered the dances
Got regularly barred from the Palais
As we eyed the girls, and weighed up our chances
With perhaps Mary, Joanna or Sally

We queued for hours to watch Tarzan
Mitchum, Cagney and Bogart – the best
At the Gaumont, ABC or the Odeon,
And on Saturday nights went 'up West'.

Brian Lynch

We saw Max Miller at the East Ham Palace,
At the Palladium we laughed at Bob Hope
Days of fun and laughter, no malice
Young years to enjoy and not mope

We fantasised about Marilyn, Jane Russell and sin
How by their pools we'd huddle and lurk
So when they found us, they'd invite us in
But on Monday we went back to work

We drank frothy coffee in the Milk Bar
Quaffed Watneys and Ind. Coope in the pubs
And yes, occasionally we did spend too far,
But what the hell - we all had a jobs

Dagenham was a bleak sort of place in those days
Barking and Ilford, where the traffic would clog,
Grimy streets, dingy shops – the memory stays
But they'd all disappear in the smog

Sometimes we did have hot weather,
And since bus services then were the best
On such days families could picnic together
In the quiet glades and peace of a forest

Some of us cheered West Ham United
In the days when Dick Walker was king
They seldom won, but we still got excited
'We're forever blowing bubbles', we'd sing

Nor will we ever forget those diabolical years
When sometimes we'd regret being born
Being bullied, the shouts and the jeers
Of Petty Officers, determined we'd conform

Still In My Own Lynchtime

We marched through the day, doing rifle drills
Never much time for slumber
Learning, by heart, our Naval skills
Not forgetting that bloody service number

I did it my way, like Frankie Sinatra once sang
Sailed the seas, and played many a field
Determined my life would go with a bang
And with real sense of purpose was filled

I'm so much older, and creakier now of course
No longer in my absolute prime
But contented, in my own mind because
I did it all – and in my own Lynchtime

Printed in the United Kingdom
by Lightning Source UK Ltd.
117316UKS00001B/216